Be Your Own Sailing Coach

"To Mum, Dad and Emily.
I could not have got through this project without you."

Be Your Own Sailing Coach

20 Goals for Racing Success

JON EMMETT

With Contributions from Paul Goodison, Simon Hiscocks and Joe Glanfield

Illustrated by Karl Brandt

WILEY NAUTICAL

John Wiley & Sons, Ltd

Other Wiley Editorial Offices

John Wiley & Sons Inc., 111 River Street, Hoboken, NJ 07030, USA

Jossey-Bass, 989 Market Street, San Francisco, CA 94103-1741, USA

Wiley-VCH Verlag GmbH, Boschstr. 12, D-69469 Weinheim, Germany

John Wiley & Sons Australia Ltd, 42 McDougall Street, Milton, Queensland 4064, Australia

John Wiley & Sons (Asia) Pte Ltd, 2 Clementi Loop   02-01, Jin Xing Distripark, Singapore 129809

John Wiley & Sons Canada Ltd, 6045 Freemont Blvd. Mississauga, Ontario, L5R 4J3

Wiley also publishes its books in a variety of electronic formats. Some content that appears in print may not
be available in electronic books.

Library of Congress Cataloging-in-Publication Data

Emmett, Jon.
Be your own sailing coach : 20 goals for racing success / Jon Emmett; with contributions from Paul
Goodison, Simon Hiscocks and Joe Glanfield.
    p. cm.
Includes index.
ISBN 978-0-470-31929-1 (pbk. : alk. paper)
1. Sailing. I. Title.
  GV811.E48 2007
  797.124--dc22   2007029093

British Library Cataloguing in Publication Data

A catalogue record for this book is available from the British Library

ISBN: 978-0-470-31929-1 (PB)

Typeset in 10/15 Futura by Thomson Digital, India
Printed and bound in Singapore by Markono Print Media Pte Ltd

Contents

Preface   ix

Introduction   xi

1   Goal Setting   1
    1.1   The importance of goal setting   2
    1.2   Smart goals   2
    1.3   Short-, medium- and long-term goals   3
    Advice from Paul Goodison   7

2   Self-preparation   9
    2.1   How prepared are you?   10
    2.2   Peaking at the correct time   11
    2.3   Checklists   13
    Advice from Simon Hiscocks   16

3   Venue Preparation   17
    3.1   Logistics   18
    3.2   Weather patterns   21
    3.3   Wind patterns   25
    Advice from Paul Goodison   30

4   Technology   31
    4.1   Keeping up with the trends   32
    4.2   Finding the perfect solution   33

4.3   Keeping it simple   33
Advice from Simon Hiscocks   34

5   Starting   37
    5.1   Time, distance and acceleration   38
    5.2   Considering wind and tide   45
    5.3   Remember the rest of the race   48
    Advice from Paul Goodison   54

6   Boat Handling   57
    6.1   Top and bottom turns   59
    6.2   Tacks and gybes   62
    6.3   Changing gear   69
    Advice from Paul Goodison   72

7   Tactics   73
    7.1   What are boat-to-boat tactics?   74
    7.2   Upwind tactics   76
    7.3   Downwind tactics   84
    Advice from Paul Goodison   92

8   Strategy   93
    8.1   What is strategy?   94
    8.2   Upwind strategy   97
    8.3   Downwind strategy   107
    Advice from Simon Hiscocks   117

9   Rules   119
    9.1   Rules: the basics   120
    9.2   Using the rules aggressively   136
    9.3   Using the rules defensively   139
    Advice from Simon Hiscocks   142

10 Meteorology   143
    10.1   Sources of weather information   144
    10.2   Understanding weather forecasts   145
    10.3   Using weather forecasts   148
    Advice from Joe Glanfield   154

11	Boat Speed: Upwind	155
	11.1 Rig set-up	156
	11.2 Making the boat 'point'	161
	11.3 Making the boat 'foot'	164
	Advice from Joe Glanfield	165
12	Boat Speed: Reaching	167
	12.1 Rig set-up	168
	12.2 'Soaking' low	169
	12.3 Going for speed	171
	Advice from Simon Hiscocks	175
13	Boat Speed: Running	177
	13.1 Rig set-up	178
	13.2 Sailing by the lee	181
	13.3 Apparent wind sailing	184
	Advice from Paul Goodison	186
14	Fitness	187
	14.1 What is fitness?	188
	14.2 How fit do you need to be?	191
	14.3 How to improve your fitness	192
	Advice from Paul Goodison	197
15	Diet	199
	15.1 Understanding nutritional labelling	201
	15.2 What we need to eat	204
	15.3 Diet suggestions	206
	Advice from Joe Glanfield	208
16	Body Weight	209
	16.1 Maintaining body weight and recovering	210
	16.2 Losing body weight	211
	16.3 Gaining body weight	212
	Advice from Joe Glanfield	214
17	Mental Attitude	215
	17.1 The importance of correct attitude	216
	17.2 Dealing with negatives	218

17.3	Relaxation techniques	219
	Advice from Joe Glanfield	221

18 Racing Log — 223
18.1	Why keep a diary?	224
18.2	How to keep good records	226
18.3	Race analysis	229
	Advice from Joe Glanfield	231

19 Concentration — 233
19.1	Looking at mental stamina	234
19.2	Maintaining focus	237
19.3	Peak concentration	240
	Advice from Joe Glanfield	241

20 Boat Preparation — 243
20.1	How prepared is your boat?	244
20.2	Dealing with boat work	247
20.3	Checklist	249
	Advice from Simon Hiscocks	250

21 Finance — 253
21.1	The true cost of sailing	254
21.2	Campaigning	256
21.3	Sponsorship	258
	Advice from Joe Glanfield	260

Glossary — 261

Index — 267

Preface

One of the reasons why it is so hard to improve your racing is that sailing is such a time-intensive sport. If you are running, you can start your training session five minutes after you've shut your front door, whereas it may take a sailor five hours (or more) to drive to the venue, fully rig the boat and get on the water. This is why full-time sailors have such an advantage over those weekend warriors. If you can sail only at weekends, it can be very unfortunate if there is too much wind to sail on the Saturday and not enough wind on the Sunday, or if, when you can sail, there is no coach available!

The aim of this book is to help those who wish to improve their skills in the shortest time possible. To achieve this you need to assess yourself and then spend your time training in the most efficient way. You can, after all, improve your sailing by going to the gym or reading (this book) from the comfort of your armchair. Coaching is an extremely important part of learning, but for the vast majority of sailors it is not possible to have a coach all the time. In fact, because of the constraints of time, money and location, many sailors may only have a coach on rare occasions.

This book is for all those busy people who still want to be successful, and need to optimise every hour of every training session without a coach!

'Flat calm or force 10. I always wear one.'

Whether they're training or out on a shout, RNLI crew members always wear lifejackets. It's a rule informed by years of experience. They know that, whatever the weather, the sea's extremely unpredictable – and can turn at a moment's notice. They see people caught out all the time. People who've risked, or even lost their lives as a result. The fact is, a lifejacket will buy you vital time in the water – and could even save your life. But only if you're wearing it.

For advice on choosing a lifejacket and how to wear it correctly, call us on 0800 328 0600 (UK) or 1800 789 589 (RoI) or visit our website rnli.org.uk/seasafety/lifejackets

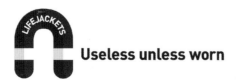

Useless unless worn

Introduction

The whole purpose of this book is to try and improve the average finishing position of the reader, whether the goal is to win at club, open, national or international level. To achieve this you need to work on your weakest areas. It may be fun to practise

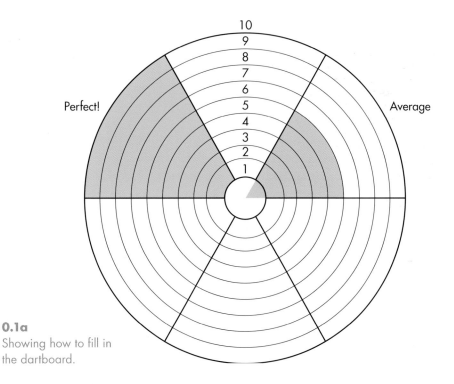

Perfect!

Average

0.1a
Showing how to fill in
the dartboard.

what you are good at, and race in your favourite conditions, but the real improvement to your overall sailing skills is to be had by working on what you are bad at. This can expand your skill base and means you have all the tools in the toolbox for when conditions change!

This book has been written so you can dip in and out of the chapters, each of which has useful exercises in it, spending time on those which are most relevant to your needs, but hopefully reading each and every one at some time.

So let's get started. First look at the dartboard (see Figure 0.1 below). You will need to rate yourself from 1 to 10 by shading in the area from the centre out – 1, in the centre, means you have no skill in that area and 10, on the outside, means you are perfect! So you need to address the topics with very little shaded in!

Devise a series of dartboards; perhaps splitting boat handling into several topics. Boat handling is an area which often causes difficulty when changing the class of boat.

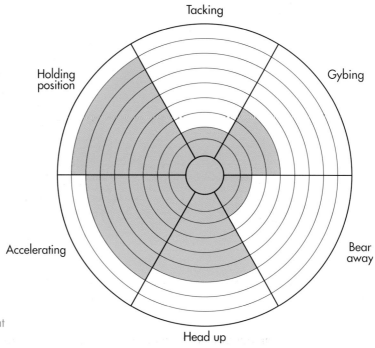

0.1b Dartboard of boat handling.

Choose one topic and break it down.

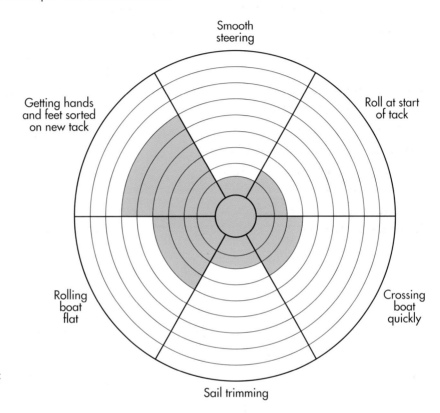

0.1c
Dartboard of tacking.

Now address the issues; maybe even producing another dartboard.

Good training is very focused, and since there are so many variables in sailing you need to ensure that you are addressing the issues most likely to improve your racing performance (not simply doing those exercises which are fun or which you are good at!). Remember, to reach a specific target may take weeks, months or even years. This is why sailing is such a difficult sport to excel in! We must often go through several 'layers'.

Each chapter has its own mini dartboard. This is simply a suggestion; you should photocopy the blank dartboard at the back of the book and make up your own targets.

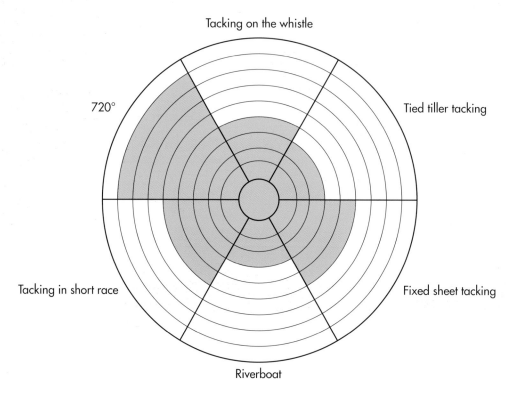

0.1d
Dartboard of actions.

You should aim to be rating yourself relatively highly in each aspect of sailing before you attend a major championship. The dartboards can be really helpful when it comes to time management!

Keep careful records of your progress so you can review your sailing in a year, or even 10 years time. Most people have inherent strengths and weaknesses, so when, for whatever reason, you have some time out of sailing, going back and working on your old problem areas will probably get you back up the pecking order sooner rather than later. Sailing is very much like riding a bike; you do not forget how to do it – but it hurts your legs more when you haven't done it for a while!

Goal Setting

The Importance of Goal Setting

Smart Goals

Short-, Medium- and Long-term Goals

Advice from Paul Goodison

1.1   The Importance of Goal Setting

There is a lot of research to show that most successful people use goal setting. This translates though many fields. Often people will not even realise they are goal setting, and may go about it in a very informal way (perhaps not even writing the goals down), but when questioned it comes to light that they were always driven towards very specific targets.

How people approach goals varies a great deal. Maybe write a key word in a prominent place, or form a star chart to show the ideas associated with a goal. Perhaps some pictures or diagrams will be useful, or get some video of top performers and try and match it. Whatever your goal, it needs to be a good goal.

1.2   Smart Goals

So what is a good goal? Well, a good goal is a SMART goal.

Specific: The more clearly defined a goal is the better, so try and be as detailed as possible. To say you want to improve boat speed is not very helpful. To say you want to improve boat speed downwind is better. However, what we are looking for is something like: improve boat speed when running in strong winds (25 knots) and flat water.

Measured: The only way you know whether you have achieved your goal is when you measure it! Some goals are easier to measure than others. For example, you want to weigh 70 kg by June, starting in January at 65 kg and putting on 1/4 kg every week. To know when you achieve your goal, you just need an accurate set of scales and to measure yourself at the same time of day (ideally first thing in the morning with an empty stomach after having been to the bathroom) in the same place (a soft or hard floor can make a difference).

Some goals are harder to measure, such as improvements in mental toughness. In these instances, you need to try and quantify items by using a scale of perceived toughness.

Agreed: Your goals may not only affect you; they may have a profound effect on your helm, crew, parents, children, wife or husband. Therefore, you need to agree any goal (possibly in writing) in order to avoid disputes over time, money or commitment. For a professional project, a formal written contract may help.

Realistic: You must not set yourself up to fail by setting a goal which is too difficult. Repeatedly failing to meet goals is very disappointing and can lead to people giving up. However, setting goals which are too easy can be equally as destructive, as there is no sense of achievement (indeed very little may have been achieved), and this too can lead to people quitting. Both extremes are examples of poor goal setting, which will ultimately mean that any dream goals are unlikely to be achieved.

Timed: A goal which may be highly unrealistic in one time frame (too easy if the time is too long, or too hard if the time is too short) may be an excellent goal in another time frame. Remember to record and monitor your goals!

Keep a detailed list of all your goals so you can refer back to them. Try and make a wide range of smart goals.

1.3 Short-, Medium- and Long-term Goals

In the previous section we looked at smart goals and noted they need to be timed.

A dream goal can be very important, as this is perhaps the goal which makes you give 100% every day. Such a goal may be to win a gold medal at the Olympics, or to be the fastest person to sail around the world. (This is often a very long-term goal). It is the short-, medium- and long-term goals that help you achieve your dream goal.

The exact length of time may vary, but generally in sailing the following applies:

Short-term goal	1–6 weeks
Medium-term goal	6 weeks–6 months
Long-term goal	over 6 months

To complete your goals, you need to assign appropriate actions. These may be completed on your own or with others. If your goal involves others, ensure that they agree to it as well, and that the aims are well laid down. Why not use the dartboard to look at your various goals and to decide which short-term goal needs to be addressed first!

Exercise:

Set six short-, three medium- and one long-term goal. The examples below will get you started.

Short:

Improve tacking in medium breeze (13–16 knots) and short chop. Action: spend a day just concentrating on tacking. Tack every three boat lengths (increase this for high performance boats) for three minutes, then rest, preferably in an onshore breeze (so it is steady). Ideally, as soon as the boat is up to full pace you tack again. The fitter the crew the longer this exercise can run. However, stop before fatigue starts to affect the tacks, as you do not want to learn bad habits. Two or three tacking sessions with high quality training sessions over a month are usually enough to see a substantial improvement.

Medium:

Depending upon your level of fitness, the time needed to get 'race fit' can vary considerably. But assuming there are no long-term illness or injury concerns, three to four months hard work can see you reach your peak fitness, or at least a substantial improvement. The end result will obviously vary from individual to individual!

A good goal may be to increase strength, for example (see Chapter 14). Following a specific training programme will lead to the desired goal (as long as it is a smart goal). Please note fitness (see Chapter 14), health (Chapter 15) and fatness (Chapter 16) are very different things!

Long:

For a long-term goal to be successful you may, first of all, have to achieve several short- and/or medium-term goals. It is important that a long-term goal is sustainable. Having spent a long time to achieve a target weight, for example, you need to make sure you do not lose it in just a couple of weeks.

A good long-term goal would be to work towards a fixed team for the future. After sailing together for a season, you decide whether you are to commit for a number of seasons (perhaps three or more) campaigning together. The top teams have one thing in common: lots of hours on the water together. However, before rushing headlong into things, you need to ensure you have the correct team. This is worth getting right first time. Remember, a group of exceptional individuals will not necessarily make an exceptional team.

Obviously, the support of a coach can be useful in all the above examples, but time and money may restrict you to having a coach only for some sessions, and therefore you need to consider for which sessions a coach would be most useful. Maybe book a number of days with a coach and chat with him or her beforehand about the goals you have, or attend some of your class training that uses the venues and coaches you believe will be the most useful for you. Different coaches have different abilities, and you need to train in venues as similar as possible to those where you will be racing.

Advice from Paul Goodison:

The best way to use goal setting is to keep it simple. I find the more complicated it gets, the harder it is to monitor and update regularly. It is useful to get a coach or friend who knows about your sailing to help you set your goals, as this way they can double-check that you are setting the right goals and help to monitor your progress. It is important to monitor your goals regularly, as this way you can record any improvements and see if you are concentrating on what you set out to achieve. If things aren't moving forward you can reassess your goals, and hopefully set new goals to move forward with. The short-term goals need to be updated regularly and should always be related to the long-term goal.

Self-preparation

How Prepared are You?

Peaking at the Correct Time

Checklists

Advice from Simon Hiscocks

2.1   How Prepared are You?

It is often said that life is about being in the right place at the right time, and this is certainly true when it comes to sail boat racing! For the key regatta of the year everything needs to be in top shape – and that includes you. The first step is to see where you are and where you want to be, and then look at how you can bridge the gap in the most efficient way!

Some elements of preparation are easy to measure. Are all the sails bought, measured and packed in the car? Can you lift a certain weight, run a certain distance in a certain time, or do X number of sit-ups? Remember, you can order several sets of identical sails/masts/foils etc., but there is still the potential for the kit to be different.

Likewise, and for no apparent reason, you may have good and bad days. On a particular day all you can do is make the best of it, and remember you can only influence things in the future.

Other elements of preparation are harder to measure, but no less important. A good example would be mental preparation. There is no point rushing around and 'getting everything done' if it leaves you

Are you fully hydrated?

tired and stressed for the regatta. Perhaps it would be better just to get the important things done, and then relax before the first race. Think: does this really need to be done now, or can it be done later?

Having said this, if a task needs to be done now, get on and do it!

Being prepared does not mean planning everything in the tiniest detail. It may be best to get up at the same time every morning when training/racing at a venue with reliable wind, but at some regattas you may have a variable start time, and therefore need to adapt your routine and adjust your plans.

When entering a regatta, try and get the notice of race early, and then register as soon as you can (assuming you are definitely planning to attend). When the race office opens try and get in quickly before there is a queue, and read the SI several times prior to any briefing, just in case there is something unusual. Often new courses and/or rules may be tested out at one or more regattas before they come into normal effect.

No two events will ever be the same, and no matter how well prepared you are, there is always the possibility of the unexpected happening. This could be boat related (the mast falling down), or something that will affect you on an emotional level. However, if you try and attend regattas which are likely to be similar, you will improve your chances of success (which is why people tend to do well sailing on their 'home waters').

Try, where possible, to be as relaxed as you are able. Be as prepared as you can be, but accept that you can never be 100%. Try not to let the unexpected phase you. It can and does happen to everyone at some time; it is how you deal with it that counts.

2.2 Peaking at the Correct Time

It is virtually impossible to be in peak condition (both physically and mentally) 365 days a year. Everyone needs some down time, and it is always best to plan this time rather than have it forced upon you! Even more important is making sure you are in peak condition at the time when it really matters.

Risk management is important when it comes to regattas. At some events you may be able to test kit, try new techniques, or really push the start line (or rule 42) so you know the limits. This is all part of getting to the very peak. Sometimes time will be too short and every event will need to be a 'counter'.

Now you may need to peak for a particular championship, perhaps the most important one for you in a year, but you also need to be racing in good enough form to make selection for

Is all the appropriate kit ready?

that event. There is no point getting to a target weight for a particular regatta if the qualification regatta will require a very different body weight. First things first!

Prior to the important regatta, train using the kit you are going to race with and try to avoid attempting any new techniques. Perhaps just do some small races and boat handling exercises to make sure you are in good form to race, as it will be too late to make large differences in boat speed. The final day before the event (if not two, for a long series), try and rest, even if light winds are forecast.

Mental skills are an important part of preparation. Are you prepared to win? If you do not think you can win, it will be very hard to do so. Has everyone in the team fully prepared? Can you help them if not? Different people deal with things in different ways and like different routines, but it is important that everyone is in the best state of mind for that key regatta.

It can actually be very hard to know when you have peaked. Often you will be on the up, but then in order to make the next jump you may have to go down a bit in performance (while trying a new technique) before you go up again. This can be viewed like a never-ending mountain range, going on and on. You just need to make sure you are near the top of your particular mountain at each regatta, and at the top of the highest mountain in the surrounding area for your key regatta.

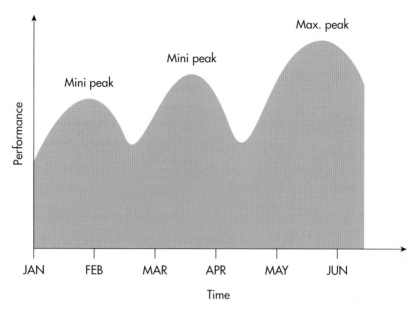

2.2 Performance hills.

2.3 Checklists

Organisation is very important: failing to plan equates to planning to fail. Remember the five Ps: Proper Preparation Produces Perfect Performance. Writing things down is not only a useful way of remembering things, but serves as a reminder when you don't!

The best advice is to sit down right now and work out all the things you need to do between now and your key regatta, the order they need to be done in and how much time it will take to achieve each task. Remember, projects can and do run over, so do not be tempted to leave vital tasks to the last minute. Figure 2.3 below shows a Gantt chart.

Keeping checklists can be very important as often the lists will be similar, and looking at old lists may prevent you from making silly but annoying mistakes. (e.g. Do apartments come with towels?)

Listing tasks that need to be done and planning a time to do them may also increase your overall efficiency. For example, if you make one trip to the chandlery

Gantt Chart: 2008 Tornado Campaign

Number	Task	Start	End	Duration	Q1 - 2008			Q2 - 2008			Q3 - 2008			Q4 - 2008	
					January	February	March	April	May	June	July	August	September	October	November
1	Tacking	1/1/2008	2/12/2008	30											
2	Gybing	1/1/2008	2/12/2008	30											
3	Hoists	2/2/2008	15/3/2008	30											
4	Drops	2/2/2008	15/3/2008	30											
5	Upwind boat speed	2/1/2008	27/9/2008	171											
6	Downwind boat speed	2/1/2008	27/9/2008	171											
7	Starting	2/1/2008	5/9/2008	70											
8	Technology	2/1/2008	5/9/2008	70											
9	Short course racing	3/1/2008	5/8/2008	48											
10	Training regattas	22/2/2008	31/10/2008	180											
11	Study rules	1/1/2008	7/8/2008	135											
12	Extra attention to diet	5/1/2008	8/8/2008	71											
13	Key regattas	7/1/2008	30/8/2008	44											
14	Reports/ major admin	30/8/2008	1/1/2009	88											
15	Rest period	9/1/2008	16/9/2008	11											
16	Sponsorship	17/9/2008	10/8/2008	15											
17	Hospitality	30/8/2008	18/10/2008	34											
18	Sell old boat/ prepare new one	9/1/2008	15/11/2008	55											
19	Fund raising	10/1/2008	6/12/2008	48											
20	Offseason fitness	11/1/2008	24/12/2008	37											

2.3 Gantt chart.

rather than several, you save time that can be better used for something else. It may also prevent the embarrassing mistake of meeting another member of your crew there, buying the same item.

So, when making lists, assign tasks to people as well as time frames. In terms of calibration setting, check and recheck that nothing has altered during travel. Never make assumptions and clearly communicate any actions to other members of the crew to ensure jobs are not done several times (too many cooks).

Where possible, have spare kit of all types. So, not only do you have a good tool box (with spares that you are likely to need for your chosen class), but also items to look after yourself – water, sun cream, food, extra clothing – so you are prepared for the possibility of long and variable days on the water. Keep lists of these items so they can be replaced before they have to be replaced. It is easier to sell good second-hand kit (and you get a better reputation) than trying to sell stuff which is on its last legs.

Advice from Simon Hiscocks:

Preparation is a huge part of any sport and it goes on and on: is your sailing kit clean, in good condition and ready to wear? Do you have the right kit for expected weather conditions? Do you know what those conditions are going to be? What kit will work in those conditions? How will you get to the venue/ airport/lift /accommodation? Something that we always do when preparing for an event is to compile a list of 'what ifs'. What happens if something goes wrong? You can then generate a solution to that problem. It's all part of covering the basics, so that come the big event the only thing to think about is performing to the best of your abilities, because that is the best anyone can ever do.

Fitness is an obvious area of self-preparation, and it is essential that a programme is followed that suits the role played on the boat. A 49er or skiff crew would want to follow a programme designed to improve aerobic fitness and strength, whilst the helm would probably pass on the strength regime and just work on the aerobic. Planning the fitness programme alongside the sailing programmes is essential to success. It takes a long time to get fit, and a short time to lose it. However, once at a level, it is relatively easy to maintain that level, so get to work early.

Weight is such a critical part of sailing boat performance that it is almost more important than fitness work: the two certainly closely interact. If your natural weight is different from your required sailing weight, it will almost certainly be of benefit to try and get to that weight as early as possible in a training period. Handling and tuning will be affected by changes in crew weight, which will affect boat speed.

Diet obviously affects fitness, weight and general energy levels, so it really does define what your body will be capable of achieving. Take away the fuel from your car and it won't run; replace it with dirty fuel and it will run badly; give it too much fuel, either clean or dirty, and it will weigh more.

Venue Preparation

Logistics

Weather Patterns

Wind Patterns

Advice from Paul Goodison

3.1 Logistics

Race strategy starts well before the first gun goes in a championship. (It could start four years before!) The aim is to get you, your boat and all your equipment to the regatta in the best shape possible. This may mean getting there very early so as to recover from jet lag and get comfortable with your surroundings, or it may mean getting there late so you can finish that all-important piece of work (which would affect your concentration), or getting in much needed quality time with friends and loved ones.

When part of a team you need to consider who is the best person on the team to handle the various responsibilities. Often the role may fall to the coaches, but perhaps their time could be better spent dealing with other issues. Parents may often handle the logistics for younger sailors (or even for older sailors with limited time!). It is important that there is open communication, as you do not want two people doing the same task!

The earlier communication can start the better: Get all the championship information for events you plan to do and book flights and ferries as early as possible (see Figure 3.1 below). This means you will have the best possible choice and will also save money. Perhaps consider driving out to a venue early to get some practice in, and then fly back for some rest so you are fit and raring to go for the championship itself.

If money is an issue, it may be better to get cheap accommodation (camping or similar) and go out early so you can get used to the venue, or else to stay home as long as possible so as to afford more comfortable accommodation. Different solutions will suit different people, and as you get older you will learn the systems that work for you

Flight booking: Your flight basket (step 3 of 5)

Your flight shopping basket for
1 adult

Change currency to:
Select Currency...

Information and options

✈ Flights

Monday 26 March

London Gatwick to Palma (Majorca)

flight 5205; dep. Mon 26 Mar 11:45
arr. Mon 26 Mar 15:00

£82.99
(per person)

NEW!

Speedy boarding

First on board, first choice of seats! Be the first to be called to board your flight for just £5.00 per person.

Saturday 07 April

Palma (Majorca) to London Gatwick

flight 5206; dep. Sat 07 Apr 16:05
arr. Sat 07 Apr 17:35

£68.99
(per person)

NEW!

Speedy boarding

First on board, first choice of seats! Be the first to be called to board your flight for just £5.00 per person.

Speedy boarding
Speedy boarding

With Speedy boarding you will be the first to be called for your flight regardless of when you check-in.

Total price for this booking will be: £10.00

Great value travel insurance from Mondial has been added automatically to your basket for your convenience and peace of mind. We strongly advise you not to travel without travel insurance. Please check the details below. You can click 'Remove' if you already have insurance or this insurance is not suitable.

⌄

Benefits for Single Trip

Cancellation & Curtailment £4,000
Medical expenses £15,000,000
Loss of passport £200

Delayed possessions £100
Personal possessions £1,500
Personal money £400
Personal

3.1 Screen shot for Flight booking (Easyjet). Courtesy of EasyJet.com.

and give the best results. Remember to keep a diary, so when you revisit a venue you know how much time and money to allow for transportation.

Once at a location it is important to be as comfortable as you can. Is it possible to eat out well – good quality and appropriate food (see Chapter 15)? Remember we are what we eat, and if we are away for a long period of time good diet becomes especially important. (You may be able to get away with one or two days of poor eating, but it will eventually catch up with you!)

Communication is important, whether it is with loved ones who cannot be with you, or to set up details for the next trip. Getting access to cheap phone calls can be very important. Skype (www.skype.com) is highly recommended as a way of making cheap calls from a computer, but you do of course need Internet access (wire-free or through Ethernet cable or similar). Also, when away from home, make sure you have the correct adapter so you can charge your electrical equipment. At the very least, ensure it is fully charged before you leave home, and perhaps take a spare mobile!

3.2 Weather Patterns

Most common venues will hold championships at the same time each year, and therefore you would expect similar conditions: light, shifty, offshore breeze or sea breeze, for example. The venues used by Olympic classes (Miami, Palma, Hyeres, Medemblik and Kiel) will be visited every year. Attending these whenever possible is a key factor, not only so they feel like a second home, but so you are also used to the weather!

The conditions at these venues will vary considerably across the year. If you have a key regatta at a venue, try and sail there the year before the championship at the same time of year. If this is not possible, train there shortly before the championship, but remember to leave yourself enough time to rest so that you are ready to race hard when the regatta starts!

To improve your sailing you need to expose yourself to as wide a number of experiences as possible. That is because by only sailing at your home club you are limiting your progress. Sailors who sail inland for years will often struggle with waves, whereas sailors who only ever sail on the sea may find it hard in flat water and light, shifting conditions.

The techniques involved in sailing in a short chop and a large rolling swell are very different. (Generally speaking, the steering matches the waves – the amount of steering matching the wave height, and the speed of steering matching the wave length.) If you are used to the wind building at around a certain time each day, you will naturally adjust your technique to suit the conditions!

For popular venues you should be able to get hold of data from the past and perhaps even a venue guide. These provide a useful starting point on which to base your strategy. However, when you go to a regatta the locals will often say, 'It is never usually like this!' It is also good to try and use the same coach, as he or she will know how best to sort you. (Some sailors like lots of weather information, whilst others prefer only that which is immediately relevant.)

If a venue usually has light or heavy winds you may even consider trying to make small changes to your body weight (see Chapter 16), so you are well suited to the expected conditions. With so many variables, a bit of study before you even get to the water may be well worthwhile!

Tide can have a huge effect on a race, so before you go for your first training session you should arm yourself with the local tidal knowledge. This will enable you to see how the tidal data relates to the course itself. Remember, tides can be affected by the weather.

Look at a chart to find the depth of the water, any channels and the flow of the water. Find a reliable source to talk to, and where possible test out any theories. Remember, the slower the boat, the greater the impact the flow of current can have. However, tide will have an effect on anything which floats on the water!

Although it is impossible to predict anything completely, tidal data tends to be very accurate. There is absolutely no reason for not trying to get tide times and tidal flows for the days of the championship, and also for any days when you are training. If you fail to do this, you can at least go out and measure the tide across the course.

−| Today |+

Date	Time	Backed	Avg Wind Direction	Veered	Min Wind Speed (Knots)	Avg Wind Speed (Knots)	Max Wind Speed (Knots)
25/03/2007	22:30.00	062	076	086	11.11	14.83	16.82
25/03/2007	22:20.00	065	072	078	13.32	15.53	17.32
25/03/2007	22:10.00	063	072	081	13.26	15.62	17.71
25/03/2007	22:00.00	067	073	081	12.74	15.49	18.44
25/03/2007	21:50.00	068	076	086	13.05	15.70	18.87
25/03/2007	21:40.00	069	082	091	13.16	16.57	19.05
25/03/2007	21:30.00	078	085	094	13.64	16.53	18.76
25/03/2007	21:20.00	078	084	092	11.89	16.11	18.61
25/03/2007	21:10.00	074	084	092	12.00	15.85	18.21
25/03/2007	21:00.00	077	085	092	13.29	16.14	18.55
25/03/2007	20:50.00	076	087	099	12.05	17.80	22.21
25/03/2007	20:40.00	085	096	103	13.57	17.92	21.79
25/03/2007	20:30.00	090	100	109	15.71	20.51	23.81
25/03/2007	20:20.00	096	104	114	16.43	20.48	24.06
25/03/2007	20:10.00	094	103	115	17.83	20.63	23.88
25/03/2007	20:00.00	096	104	113	16.50	21.06	25.70
25/03/2007	19:50.00	096	105	117	17.19	20.42	24.22
25/03/2007	19:40.00	098	106	114	17.38	20.25	23.91
25/03/2007	19:30.00	093	103	111	16.66	19.83	23.47
25/03/2007	19:20.00	091	099	108	16.94	20.83	24.86
25/03/2007	19:10.00	092	100	109	18.10	22.00	25.57
25/03/2007	19:00.00	092	105	116	18.11	22.56	27.63
25/03/2007	18:50.00	097	105	117	14.84	19.36	23.19
25/03/2007	18:40.00	098	105	115	14.19	18.58	22.45
25/03/2007	18:30.00	101	109	116	13.79	18.52	22.04
25/03/2007	18:20.00	100	109	120	15.99	18.80	21.15
25/03/2007	18:10.00	102	111	119	15.10	18.23	21.16
25/03/2007	18:00.00	102	107	117	16.63	18.60	20.80
25/03/2007	17:50.00	103	111	120	15.65	18.54	20.77
25/03/2007	17:40.00	100	110	124	14.35	18.49	21.66
25/03/2007	17:30.00	101	110	126	14.07	18.10	21.16
25/03/2007	17:20.00	095	104	118	12.92	18.87	22.01
25/03/2007	17:10.00	098	104	113	15.46	19.58	22.59
25/03/2007	17:00.00	095	103	112	15.15	20.29	23.94
25/03/2007	16:50.00	095	104	118	15.66	20.23	23.13
25/03/2007	16:40.00	096	103	112	14.91	18.76	23.05
25/03/2007	16:30.00	096	105	116	15.85	18.99	22.56
25/03/2007	16:20.00	100	109	121	15.11	20.31	23.90
25/03/2007	16:10.00	098	108	123	15.38	18.66	22.19
25/03/2007	16:00.00	102	111	123	14.91	21.08	25.35
25/03/2007	15:50.00	107	117	127	18.47	22.42	25.98
25/03/2007	15:40.00	108	119	129	15.30	20.59	24.97
25/03/2007	15:30.00	110	119	126	15.13	18.63	22.19
25/03/2007	15:20.00	105	117	128	13.35	16.36	19.82
25/03/2007	15:10.00	099	108	120	11.67	15.94	19.21
25/03/2007	15:00.00	098	107	118	10.31	15.42	19.47
25/03/2007	14:50.00	100	109	117	12.56	14.90	17.01
25/03/2007	14:40.00	090	099	107	13.95	16.58	18.77
25/03/2007	14:30.00	085	096	113	12.10	15.26	20.14
25/03/2007	14:20.00	062	085	104	8.81	11.64	16.90
25/03/2007	14:10.00	055	066	074	9.72	12.44	15.44
25/03/2007	14:00.00	051	060	072	10.89	13.97	16.85

3.2a Wind data for a venue. Courtesy of WeatherFile.com.

Your EasyTide Prediction (free)

○ PORTLAND, England
Port predictions (Standard Local Time) are equal to UTC

Daylight saving: 0 hours

see daylight saving warning

Start Date: Today – Sunday 25th March 2007 (Standard Local Time)
Duration: 1 day

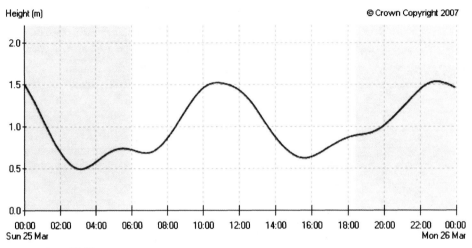

Height (m)   © Crown Copyright 2007

Sun 25 Mar

LW	HW	LW	HW
03:28	10:44	15:55	22:56
0.4 m	1.5 m	0.5 m	1.5 m

Predicted heights are in metres above Chart Datum

Daylight Saving Warning: EasyTide predictions are based on the standard time of the country concerned. For the UK this is GMT and the daylight saving offset should be set to 1 hour to allow for British Summer time (from 01:00 am on Sunday 25th March 2007 until 02:00am on 28th October 2007).

3.2b Tidal data for a venue. Courtesy of Crown Copyright.

3.3 Wind Patterns

There is no point being the fastest guy on the race course if you are going in the wrong direction. Not only do you need to sail fast, you need to sail smart: 'get your head out of the boat' and look around. Remember, winds tend to vary from forecasts.

There may be patterns in the wind forced by topography. Look at the surrounding area. Google Earth is a great way to do this. If the wind is offshore, it will most likely be shifty, but how shifty will depend upon how much land there is, how high the land is near the shore and how close to the shore the race course is. Race committees will often use the same sailing area, so getting to know the various wind patterns is extremely useful.

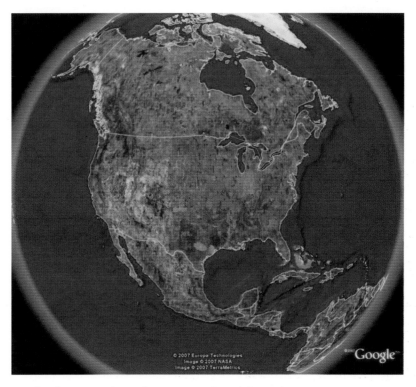

3.3a Screen shot from Google earth. Courtesy of Google Earth.

When the wind is blowing approximately parallel to the land there can be big differences in the wind on the race course. When the land is on your left and the wind is on your right, for example:

- a south-facing coast with an easterly breeze;
- a north-facing coast with a westerly breeze;
- an east-facing coast with a northerly breeze;
- or a west-facing coast with a southerly breeze

there is more breeze near land. Rotate the upper diagram in figure 3.3b to match your shoreline. This is because the wind coming off the land is converging with the wind on the water (wind coming off the land is at a slightly different angle). The area of greater wind will vary but can often be up to 25% stronger than the wind offshore.

When the land is on your right and the wind is on your left, for example:

- a south-facing coast with a westerly breeze;
- a north-facing coast with an easterly breeze;
- an east-facing coast with a southerly breeze;
- or a west-facing coast with a northerly breeze

there is less breeze near land. Rotate the lower diagram in figure 3.3b to match your shoreline. This is divergence, where the wind coming off the land is separating from the wind off the water (wind coming off the land is at a slightly different angle). The area of lesser wind will vary but can often be up to 25% lighter than the wind inshore.

The extent of this area of stronger and weaker wind will depend upon the size of the landmass. (The above rules apply in the northern hemisphere; it is completely the opposite in the southern hemisphere!)

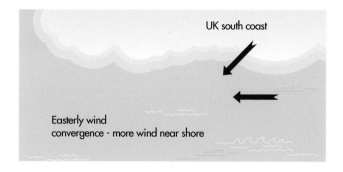

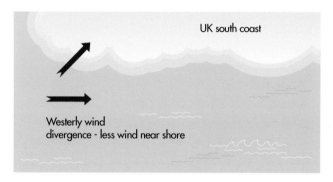

3.3b Wind diagrams showing convergence and divergence.

Any offshore breeze see Figure 3.3c will result in a shifty wind, so there could well be no pattern. If this is the case, it means sailing to the compass to keep sailing on a lift, and where possible remaining in the centre of the race course. If you can, pre start information about the size and frequency of any shifts, so you know what the average wind shift is. The closer you get to shore, the greater the frequency and size of the shifts. There wind direction will be slightly to the right over the land, with an area of stronger wind (as long as the wind direction remains the same) near the coast, but very light winds just by the coast. Therefore, it may well pay to take the tack which takes you inshore to get into more wind and/or sail the starboard tack first to take advantage of the wind bend.

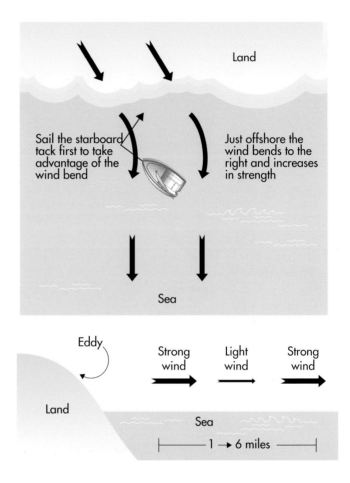

Sail the starboard tack first to take advantage of the wind bend

Just offshore the wind bends to the right and increases in strength

Land

Sea

Eddy

Strong wind

Light wind

Strong wind

Land

Sea

1 → 6 miles

3.3c Offshore winds.

Sea breezes see figure 3.3d can also make a big difference. In the northern hemisphere the wind will continually go right. Sea breeze will usually develop by the afternoon with cumulus clouds forming around 11:00 (which could well be the time you launch). A small onshore breeze will develop where the cold air is sucked in to replace the warm air rising off the land. A good sea breeze can often reach 20 knots a couple

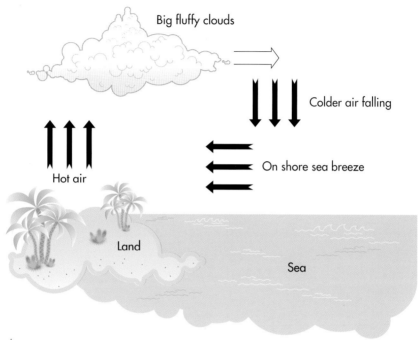

Big fluffy clouds

Colder air falling

Hot air

On shore sea breeze

Land

Sea

3.3d Sea breeze.

of hours after it starts. Normal sea breeze is just (perhaps) 15 knots left of 90 degrees to the coast (roughly southerly on a south coast). It will then clock around 10 degrees an hour until it dies off an hour or so before dusk. Unfortunately, a gradient breeze can stop a sea breeze, so the sooner this dies the better, as it will oppose the sea breeze either at the top or the bottom of the circulation.

Ideally, on each race day, the coach will go out and monitor the wind in terms of speed, direction, frequency of gusts/lulls and current tidal situation, as well as looking out for the start of a sea breeze. However, you may have to be your own coach! Get out early and, if at all possible, make some notes. (Use Wet Notes, or even write on the boat itself!)

Advice from Paul Goodison:

Preparation is the key to success! If you fail to prepare, you are preparing to fail.
    When gathering information on a venue it is important to decide how useful the information will be and how reliable the source of the information is. I always try to use information that I trust, from a person I respect, such as a coach or a fellow sailor who's a friend. I try and avoid the local fishermen, as the information may be relevant for fellow fishermen, but maybe not for sailors. If there are recurrent trends, try and check them out while practising to validate the information. Don't just take it as gospel in the first race. Be careful when getting information from other classes, as what may work in a 49er could be very different from what will work in a Laser, due to the characteristics of the boats. I try to sail in the racing area a few days prior to the regatta to gain as much information as possible that will help when racing starts.

Technology

Keeping up with the Trends

Finding the Perfect Solution

Keeping it Simple

Advice from Simon Hiscocks

4.1 Keeping up with the Trends

There is no doubt that by not having the best equipment you are making it harder to perform. Finance may be the factor, and so as the return for your investment diminishes you may choose to drop out of the arms race. You should always be aware (even if not following them) of the latest trends.

Often people just keep up with the trends because they want to be on a level playing field. Not every trend which goes around the boat park will make the boat go faster or any easier to sail. When doing initial testing, often only one out of ten tests will be better than the original – and that is if you are lucky.

Box of ropes, polish, lubricant etc. – very useful!

Try and avoid having kit you can blame when things go wrong. Remember, you are only as good as your weakest link. Even kit which is going to have a positive advantage needs time to get used to. In difficult regattas it is often people who know their kit the best (and how to get the best out of it) who win, as opposed to those with the best kit.

4.2   Finding the Perfect Solution

Often the perfect solution does not exist, so time and money could be better spent elsewhere. However, you do need to work towards the best solution, given the resources available.

The only way to make an objective decision is to weigh up the pros and cons, and try and quantify perceived benefits as far as possible. Would money be best spent buying another set of sails, sailing a regatta, or trying to develop new sails?

Having a good training partner can make a real difference. This may be someone you work with who shares costs, or it may even be someone from outside the class whom you pay. They need to be reliable and consistent in their approach and performance, so any difference (either positive or negative) can be easily seen. This may require patience, and perhaps the presence of a third party to help analyse the differences.

4.3   Keeping it Simple

When you start sailing a new class of boat the best piece of advice is to keep it simple. Copy the equipment, set-ups and techniques of the leading boats (perhaps the National Champion) and you give yourself an excellent starting point!

Technology needs to be reliable if it is to be useful. If you are not sure of the reliability, keep lots of spares.

When making changes you need to make them one at a time, so you know exactly what the difference is. Record variations in as much detail as possible: you may find some information, which at the time seemed insignificant, useful to refer back to later.

Try and keep the same principles when changing class, transferring the same equipment from boat to boat as much as possible, so that it is familiar to you. If you are making developments, try and do this in the off season, when there are not so many regattas, so you can give it your full attention and can see the project through to completion.

Advice from Simon Hiscocks:

Like it or not, sailing is an equipment sport, and that equipment plays an important role in racing performance. Every boat will, to a certain extent, have an element of technological development or potential that may affect performance. How it is used is the crucial factor in how it might affect overall performance.

Tool Kit, power drill, spare blocks are essential.

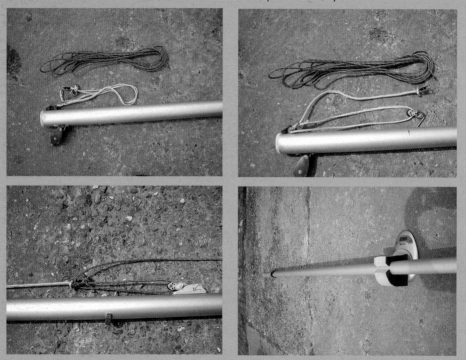

Good rigging is essential: measure spar stiffness (shown here by weighing) and control line lengths.

The base level is to get the standard kit, or kit that is known to be competitive. Anything above this is to gain a little bit on the competition. Rarely do people make large jumps in performance: the gains are generally the cumulative effect of small improvements.

Ultimately the question must be asked: is there any technology that can help us? It may not be something that directly affects on-the-water racing. It may be, for instance, to use a GPS tracking device in practice events to try and analyse decision-making. Or to ensure that all the crew has identical, calibrated scales to check body weight. Technology can be used in a variety of imaginative ways that might ultimately help a team's performance.

Check your mast rake (shown here by measuring).

It is always worth considering how much a piece of technology is likely to help, and whether it is worth it. Would you be better off with some newer sails or a new mast, rather than a fancy compass or a special lightweight gizmo? How much time will it employ? And could this time be better spent on the water training?

Viewing a campaign in terms of levels, where the bottom level is the basic competitive boat and anything above that is a bonus, what do the champions, at the level you are aiming at, have? If the basic boat is below this level, draw up a priority list that defines what it is most important to get hold of, or do, to close that gap. It is worth looking at the level you are aiming at, for it might be that the World Champion spends a lot of money on a potentially tiny advantage just because he/she perceives that it helps his/her mind set. For the National title or the club trophy, it will make not the blind bit of difference. (Nor, for that matter, will it make a difference for the World title.) So be careful of the blind alleys.

Starting

Time, Distance and Acceleration

Considering Wind and Tide

Remember the Rest of the Race

Advice from Paul Goodison

5.1 Time, Distance and Acceleration

Quite simply, how good your start is can have a major impact on how good your finish is! With the number of discards low in most series, we can rarely afford a bad start. Starting can form a very large percentage of the race. Obviously, in conditions when you are particularly fast, the importance of a start will diminish (just do not get OCSed), but being able to start well is definitely a skill worth having, especially when competing in competitions with shorter courses, or where one side of the first beat is heavily favoured. The better you are at starting, the more difficult the starts you can attempt in a regatta situation. As with all practical skills, practice makes perfect!

All boats behave differently, and this varies as the racing area changes. (Some boats will quickly become overpowered, while others are usually underpowered.) However, the principles remain the same for single-handers, high performance boats, catamarans, yachts and everything in between (for example, boats accelerate quicker in flatter water) and so do the techniques (to get the boat up to speed). When joining a new class one of the most important things to do, is to learn how to get off the start line in good shape. Remember, a good start is one where you have clean wind, go in the direction you want and where you can hold your lane 30 seconds after the gun. Three seconds after the gun it is often not clear who has had a good start!

The exact roles within the boat will depend upon the class you sail, but it is important that you are adequately prepared (see Chapter 2) before you even approach the start line. In a boat with more than one crew, it is well worth sitting the whole team down to make a list of all the tasks to be done and the order in which to do them. Now distribute the tasks, so all the members can list the actions they need to take, and then everyone can compare. It will often come as a great surprise to see how many things need to be achieved to get a good start!

Even if you are familiar with the class and race area, it is worth going out early to practise getting the boat up to full pace, and seeing how long this takes you in terms of time and distance. The set-up for the start may also vary slightly from the set-up for the first beat, so you may need to ensure your rig set-up is suitable for the conditions. (Note: you may need to put slightly more power in the sails to cope with the confused water around the starting area.) If there are any issues, then the earlier you launch, the more time you have to rectify any mistakes.

The time it takes to accelerate depends upon the class of boat, but all boats accelerate best around their 'designed wind'. This is usually medium airs (around 14 knots), with high performance boats getting powered up sooner than lower performance boats. In these conditions, the sails are fully powered up, but the boat is not overpowered (so crew weight obviously has an impact here). If the breeze is noticeably lighter or stronger than this, the boat will be less efficient and so will take longer to get up to full speed for the conditions. In terms of tuning the boat for acceleration, a good basis is to set the boat for medium airs, then work up or down until things are set for the day's conditions.

Exercise 1: Time

How easy is it to remain sitting on the line, without drifting to leeward or ending up head to wind? Remember, as a windward boat you need space to leeward to get off the line in good shape, but more importantly you must be careful not to make contact with a leeward boat, as the last thing you want to be doing is exonerating yourself at start time.

Find a buoy. Start as close as you can, either with the mark to windward or leeward, and hold position for as long as possible.

Buoy to Windward:

Start right next to the buoy; the boat will slowly drift to leeward (the exact speed depending upon the conditions). When you are two boat lengths from the buoy, put in two tacks and start again (if the buoy is to windward).

To tack without going over the line, sheet in as little as possible to get the boat moving, overemphasise the steering and, if possible, back the main by pushing the boom out.

When you pass, head to wind. (This will stop you going forwards, as well as helping you turn.) To get the bow down, back the jib by pulling in the 'wrong' sheet. With a self-tacking jib, literally pull it to windward.

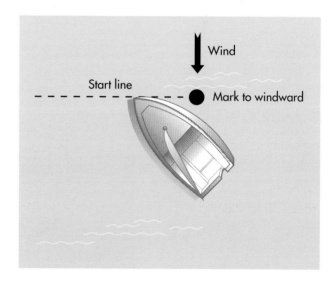

5.1a Holding station with a buoy to windward.

Buoy to Leeward:

Start two boat lengths from the buoy and stay on the line for as long as possible. Once you get to the point where you could no longer sail over the line (DO NOT HIT THE

BUOY!), reverse out, and sail back to your original starting position. To reverse, put the boat head to wind and push the boom as far forward as it will go. Remember, as you start to go backwards you have no rights and the steering will be acting in reverse!

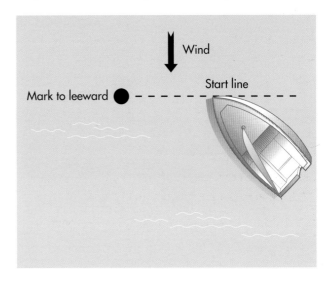

5.1b Holding station with a buoy to leeward.

In both starts you must not go over the line (pretend it is a black flag start).

Top Tips:

Keep the boat flat to stop it going sideways. (If, for some reason, you wish to go sideways, simply lift the centreboard.) If you end up going head to wind, release some kicker. When you go backwards you need to keep the weight well forward to stop the transom from digging in.

Exercise 2: Acceleration

To practise acceleration, find two other boats of similar ability. Line up, completely stationary, with one boat length between boats, and all boats an equal distance upwind. The boat in the middle loudly shouts, '3, 2, 1, GO!', and accelerates up to full speed upwind. As soon as the boats are up to speed, stop and change

positions. There is no need to wait until one boat pops out of the front or back: this is not the purpose of the exercise. The leeward boat becomes the windward boat; the other two boats remain still so the old windward boat is now in the middle, calling the start, and the previous middle boat is now to leeward.

To help the boat get up to pace, you need to bear away. Get the boat to bear away without going forward (by using the rudder but not allowing the sail to fill), so the boat does not go over the imaginary line, but is in a good position to accelerate easily. This is often referred to as getting the bow down.

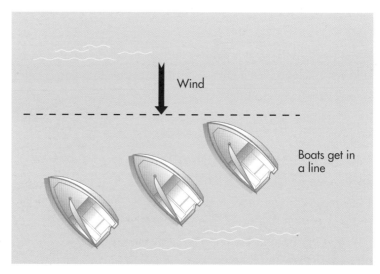

5.1c Three boat trigger pulling.

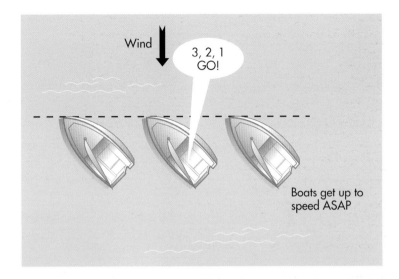

5.1c (Continued)

Top Tip:

It may pay to set the rig up for slightly more power than you will need upwind, so you can keep your height and not fall into the boat to leeward of you. This also helps if the wind and waves are very disturbed around the starting area.

Exercise 3: Distance

In an ideal world you will hit the line at full speed. You need to know how much space this will take. The class of boat will make a big difference, but so will the conditions. However, remember both the wind and the water are likely to be confused around the starting area, so it may well take more distance than you think to get up to full speed. On your own, start next to a buoy, and from stationary see how long it takes you to get up to full speed. Now go back to the line and start the same distance back. See if you have the distance about correct.

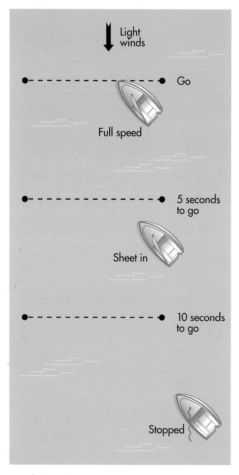
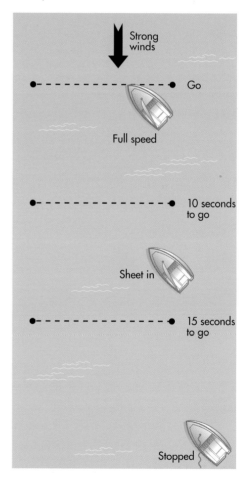

5.1d Timed run.

Top Tip:

Monitor the difference in distances when the wind lulls/gusts, so that near start time you never get too far from the start line. The boat will accelerate best when starting on a close reach.

When considering your start, remember that the closer you are to the favoured end, the greater your advantage (regardless of what is causing that advantage), but also the more crowded this part of the line is likely to be. If you are over, it is easy to go round the ends. However, in a black flag situation you need to be especially careful, as you are going to be more likely to have your numbers recorded. It is also possible that the favoured end of the line may not be the favoured side of the beat (for example, you may start at the port end and wish to go right, or start at the starboard end and go left). If you are not confident of getting a good start and going the best way up the beat, you need to consider which is the more important factor.

5.2   Considering Wind and Tide

Assuming that the wind remains constant in strength and direction, and there is no current or difference in the waves, the favoured end of the line is the part which is most upwind.

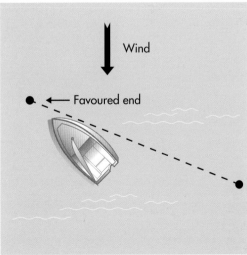

5.2a Favoured end of the line due to wind angle.

This mark is also the favoured mark to round if the start line is a downwind gate (as this mark and the windward mark are closer to each other than the other end of the line and the windward mark). The simplest method is to go head to wind on the line and see which end of the line you are pointing at. This is much better than sailing up and down the line, which may be difficult to do accurately, complicated by the presence of other boats and with a large line may well take some time.

In reality, the wind is often oscillating, which means that the favoured end of the line may continually change. In this case you do not want to commit yourself to starting at one end of the line too early. (With a long line you may not be able to get down to the new favoured end if there is a large wind shift.) If there is a regular pattern you may well be able to predict what the wind is going to do at/shortly before/shortly after start time. (Try and get to the starting area early and track what the wind is doing.) Please note that if the windward mark is slightly offset to the left or right, this in no way affects the line bias; it simply means that you will spend more time on one tack than the other!

Over the course of a day the tide will no doubt vary considerably. For example, the current may have no effect on the first race of the day when the wind is strong and the current is weak, but may be at the end of the day the current is the most important

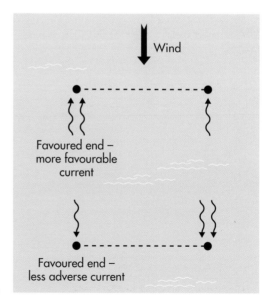

5.2b Favoured end of the line due to current.

factor when the wind has dropped and the current has increased. You should expect to look at the predicted tides for a regatta before you even drive to the venue!

If the line is square to the wind you want to start at the end with the most favourable current (being careful not to be over) or the least adverse current (remembering it will be harder to hold your position on the line).

If the current is flowing parallel to the line it makes no difference to the line bias. However, the end of the line the current is flowing to is likely to be very crowded, so if everything else is equal you should aim to start at the other end (up current). If the current is strong, boats at the extreme ends may not be able to get across the line.

There could also be a difference in wind strength across the course, resulting in one side being favoured, perhaps due to wind funnelling around a landmass.

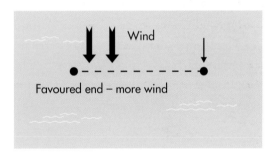

5.2c Favoured end of the line due to wind strength.

If the wind and current are equal across the race course, but there are differences in waves, head for the area where you can sail fastest: to sail faster upwind try and sail

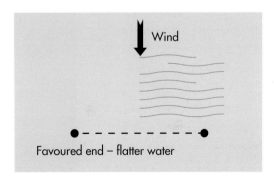

5.2d Favoured end due to wave size.

in flat water. Downwind, if you can surf (downwind in a Laser, for example), the waves may help you sail faster. However, if you are planing freely (for example, in a 49er), waves will slow you down and you should avoid them.

You need to weigh up the current conditions (and future predictions) when choosing where to start on the line. Remember, being a small way down from the favoured end will probably make it easier to find some space to accelerate into. After the race, try and sit down to work out whether you feel you made the correct decision – and always try and learn from your mistakes! You will find that you will visit some venues repeatedly, and that the race area, dates of the regatta and start times may well be similar.

5.3 Remember the Rest of the Race

The start is the beginning of the race, not the end. There is no point winning the port end of the line if you miss the first shift. When lots of boats are being OCSed, a more cautious approach may be advisable as, especially early on in the series, it may not be

worth risking a race disqualification. Often it may be obvious when a race is likely to be general recalled; this is not the time to push the line hard!

When looking at the start you must consider the first beat. If one side of the race course is heavily biased, due to differences in wind speed (more wind) or angle (a wind bend) or strong current difference across the race course, it may well be worth considering starting away from what you would consider the favoured end of the line (see Figure 5.3a–d) to ensure you can work the favoured side of the beat!

Probably the most difficult place to start is in the very middle of the line, as here it is hardest to know when you are on the line. This accounts for the common mid-line sag.

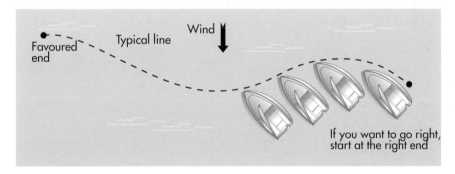

5.3a Middle line sag.

What you really need is some transits: two objects lined up that tell you whether you are on the line or not. If you are confident in your position you may even be able to start on port! Transits may be taken from in front or behind, and need to be two large and immoveable objects.

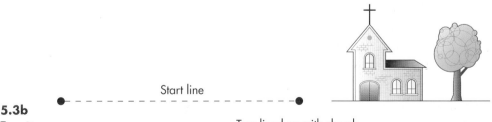

5.3b
Transits.

Tree lined up with church.

The following exercise is a good way to practise using transits:

Exercise 4: The Transit Exercise

The coach boat is anchored and the sailors sail up to the middle of the line (the longer the line is, the harder the exercise). When, and only when, the boat is stationary, the sailors raise a hand and the coach can then inform them whether they are on/over or behind the line. Ideally, the exercise is repeated until the sailors are consistently on the line.

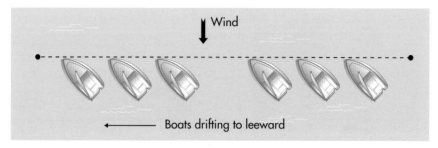

5.3c Lining up in the group (drifting sideways).

Top Tip:

When sitting on the line you need to see along a straight edge. Looking down the bowsprit or down the tiller (when in the centre) can work very well. If the helm is on the line, often you are a half a boat length over.

Starting at Port or Starboard End

When you start at the pin end you need to be careful. If you start right by the buoy it is possible that you may not be able to get over the line at all with a bad start. The best way is often to come in from port on port and find a gap, somewhere along the line.

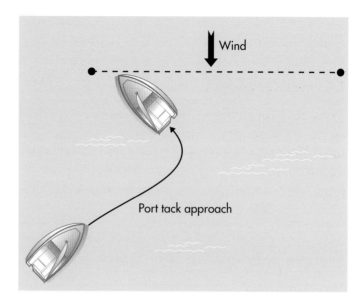

5.3d Port tack approach.

It may be possible to be the closest boat to the pin, but often it will be safer to find a natural gap along the line. Look how the line is building and time your approach accordingly. If you have to duck boats, being on port is an advantage as the other boats on starboard will be moving slightly, so you will pass more boats than you would if you had to sail under them on starboard.

Starting at the starboard end may be quite difficult. Often a large committee boat will have a large wind shadow, and if you are over you are likely to get your numbers taken. You will need to choose early how close to the end you wish to start. Often this is dictated by how soon you wish to tack after the start. (If you have to go right you may even consider

risking a second row start if it guarantees you will be among the first to tack!) See how quickly you drift sideways and line up so you will be where you wish to be at start time. Quality fleets may line up quite early, and there is unlikely to be much room if the line is quite biased. Think: is it a day when a gap is likely to appear?

Top Tip:

The more kicker you have on, the more the boat will want to go head to wind. The more kicker you let off, the more the boat will slip sideways. Try and find a balance point, which is usually about halfway between kicker fully off and the kicker you will be using on the beat.

Exercise 5: Protecting Your Space

Keeping your gap to leeward is vital: you need the space to accelerate into. When everyone is looking for a space to start, you need to protect your gap (shutting the door). Keep the bow off the wind (below close hauled course); the boom is now out (the sails are flapping) – this closes the gap. If any sailors come in to leeward, they must give you room to keep clear. As you head up to avoid them

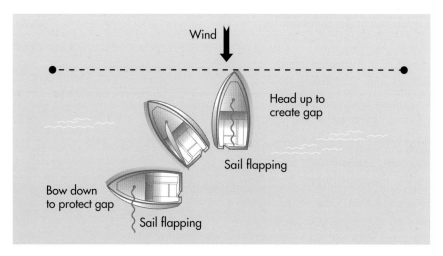

5.3e Protecting the gap.

you will still have room (although the hole will now be smaller). To create space or to make it larger, work the boat up to above close hauled course (without sheeting in the sails).

For the start, make any final rig changes before you bear away. Use the jib to help you do this before the gun and go down to below close hauled course, allowing your sails to fill on a close reach. (As soon as the boat is up to speed you may return to a close hauled course.) If you do not have a jib, you will need to use the rudder to bear away. Pull the tiller towards you hard, gently push it away and then pull it hard towards you again. Ensure that the bow is bearing away and you are not making the boat go forward (as this would break rule 42).

Top Tip:

If you do lose your space, try and look for another one early – if there is still time. Sometimes you will be forced to start in a difficult place, but often there is a better alternative. Once you are completely stationary or head to wind, it is very hard to manoeuvre, so avoid this if possible.

Whatever happens, as soon as the gun has gone, concentrate on getting your boat up to maximum speed. Now 'get your head out of the boat' to consider your options (carry on or tack), as these early decisions will make a big impact on your race – and remember, keep trying! Sailing is a dynamic sport and it is possible to recover from a poor start. It is often these races (not your best ones) which decide the outcome of a championship. You can discuss what went wrong (or right!) with the start after the race. Keeping good records is vital. You may even choose to use a regatta as a 'practice regatta', so as to test your starts – often two OCSs in a regatta could be disastrous.

Advice from Paul Goodison:

- Become comfortable with the conditions. I sail most of the beat before the start sequence to gain confidence in my boat speed and set-up.

- Devise a plan and strategy: which way do I want to go up the beat? And where do I want to start?

- Once the line is set, look for transits and decide how valuable they might be.

- Once the warning signal has sounded, it's time to double-check the transit and line bias.

- Get ready to synchronise the watch at the preparatory signal.

- Sail upwind again to double-check the set-up and the line bias. Leaving the sail controls set in the upwind settings but with the kicker eased, return behind the line. Leaving the kicker eased stops the boat from accelerating when hovering.

- At the 1 minute signal, check the timing again and get in position for the final approach. This may need to be done earlier in larger fleets when the line is heavily biased.

- Try to maintain sight of one end of the line at all times, so as to be able to gauge your position.

- You need to be aware of what is happening around, especially boats entering from astern that may steal the gap to leeward.

- With 25 seconds to go, start to create a gap to leeward. Any earlier than this and the gap will be open for others.

- With 10 seconds to go, pull the kicker on and start to pull the bow down to accelerate.

- With 3 seconds to go, the boat should be up to speed ready to hit the line with pace.

- When accelerating, bring the bow down below close hauled as this will help to accelerate, and create flow around the foils, which stops the boat slipping sideways.

- The first 30 seconds after the start are the most critical. All concentration should be on boat speed and holding the lane. Don't look round or fiddle with controls until advanced on the boats around.

- The key to good starts is confidence in your ability and confidence in where the line is, so you can attack it flat out knowing that you are not over.

Boat Handling

Top and Bottom Turns

Tacks and Gybes

Changing Gear

Advice from Paul Goodison

A ny boat will probably be sailing fastest when using minimal corrective steerage (that is, when the rudder is not acting as a brake). Even in classes like the Laser where you do lots of turns downwind, if you can do this with minimal rudder movement (and a nice flat boat when sailing in a straight line) you will be quick. (If the boat is too heeled you end up using the rudder just to keep it in a straight line.) Even when turning corners, the less you use the rudder as a brake the better! However fast a boat is, it is still important to minimise steering where possible, using the boat balance and sail trim to turn the boat, and allowing the rudder just to follow on behind.

Boat handling drills are the key to any successful campaign. You need to be able to get your boat around the race course before you start to race. When you first start high performance sailing you need to sort out your boat handling in under 15 knots before you go out in 25! Until your boat handling is sorted it will often be more productive (in terms of your long-term development)

to work on boat handling than to go racing. You cannot race effectively if your boat handling is not up to scratch; it will impact on your race tactics and strategy.

Undoubtedly the best way to improve all aspects of boat handling is that old cliché: 'time on the water'. However, the more specific and demanding you make the exercises, the greater the potential gains. It is also good to change exercises to add variety and keep motivation to train high. Once good boat handling has been achieved, you can rediscover key skills very quickly after a reasonable break. Boat handling routines can also be a good way of developing specific fitness, for example by doing lots of spinnaker hoists and drops.

Boat handling skills are required at low speed (little wind) and high load (when just hit by a gust). It is not all about acceleration and top speed. Being able to slow down, hold position and turn without going forward are all vital skills on the race course. Boat handling skills really cover any type of sailing which isn't sailing in a straight line. Land-based drills are a vital part of boat handling development as you can slow tasks down, stop in the middle and think about what you are doing (without risking a capsize or getting stuck head to wind).

Having good boat handling means that you have all the tactical options: you can tack under someone, knowing you will come out with good speed and not get rolled, or you can leave the gybe right to the lay line, knowing you can put the gybe in quickly and exactly where you want to. Just think how many tacks and gybes you could make in the average race day. If you could make each one 1/3 of a boat length better, that would add up to quite a few places when you think how close the fleet usually finish.

6.1 Top and Bottom Turns

When sailing downwind and going fast, you are always looking for the gap in the waves – the space in the wave of least resistance – so you can carry on surfing without loading up the rig. Obviously you cannot always be surfing, but in conditions where you can, you want to hold the surf for as long as possible. It takes far less energy to keep the boat surfing than it does to get it to surf in the first place. Even in conditions where you can go over the waves, you are always looking for the flattest point to cross.

When you start jumping waves, you need to be careful that you do not go clean over a wave and then bury your bow in the wave in front. (Sometimes you have to slow down to stay upright.)

There will come a point when there is enough speed to go straight over the waves (and indeed there is a point where it is not worth steering as you can not catch the waves). At that stage you go straight to the mark. However, in these conditions there tends to be less difference in speed, hence the importance of working on top and bottom turns. This is also true when you do not have enough speed to catch the waves (or the waves are too small to catch), when you are more or less pointing at the mark (just looking to stay in the pressure).

The key point is to find a sitting position where the boat is finely balanced. Now only small movements will allow you to change the boat's direction. If you find yourself always leaning in (or out) then something is wrong with your sitting position. (Or maybe with your rig set-up – check: are you over or under powered?)

6.1a To get the boat to head up you need to put in some leeward heel and sheet in the main.

6.1b To get the boat to bear away you need to put in some windward heel and sheet out the main.

6.1c When the boat has reached the desired direction, you need to set the heel and sheeting so the boat continues in a straight line (do the opposite of what you did to start the turn).

Example:

The breeze is dropping, so you move your weight right in and sheet in slightly to head up into more wind. Allow the rudder simply to follow the boat. As you get into more pressure, you sit on the side and the boat comes flat and accelerates (the sheet is already in, so no need to sheet). Now bear away to stay in the gust by sheeting out, and the boat will come slightly on top of you. When it is going in its new desired direction sit in slightly so the helm is neutral.

The more kicker you apply, the easier it is for the boat to head up. (Think: you often have more kicker on upwind than down.) The closer the course you are sailing is to a reach, the more kicker you need. The least kicker you need is on the run (although you always need some), so the leach returns after opening. (You also need some kicker for tapered masts to support the top of the mast!) If you are making turns downwind and then holding the angle for a bit (going high in the lulls and low in the gusts), it may well be worth 'playing' (constantly adjusting) the kicker.

6.2   Tacks and Gybes

The exact movement of your hands and feet will be very similar for both, regardless of the conditions. What will change is the speed and timing (see 6.3).

A good tack is a tack where you continue to make maximum progress upwind. The aim is not to tack as quickly as possible, or to come out as fast as possible, but to continue getting closer to the windward mark as fast as you can. The boat may then (as a result) spend a reasonable amount of time head to wind (going a bit slower, but in exactly the right direction). This obviously depends upon the class and the sailing conditions.

A good gybe run to run follows the same principle. You wish to make as much ground downwind as possible.

There may be times when you have to tack or gybe quickly, so it is important to practise this occasionally. However, priority should be given to doing 'good' tacks and gybes. Remember, the slower the turn the easier it is to get across the boat, but the slower the boat may end up going, so be careful not to load up the rig. Generally you want to turn as fast as you can with good crew movements.

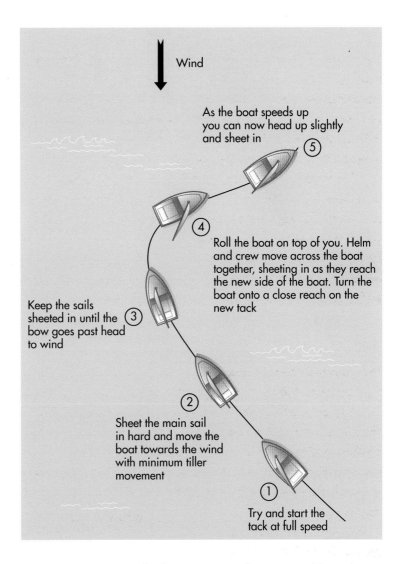

Wind

As the boat speeds up you can now head up slightly and sheet in ⑤

Roll the boat on top of you. Helm and crew move across the boat together, sheeting in as they reach the new side of the boat. Turn the boat onto a close reach on the new tack ④

Keep the sails sheeted in until the ③ bow goes past head to wind

Sheet the main sail in hard and move the boat towards the wind with minimum tiller movement ②

Try and start the tack at full speed ①

6.2a Best course to sail when tacking.

Reach to reach gybing is about getting the boat going as fast as possible in the new direction as quickly as possible. On a windy day it may be safer to do a run to run gybe, and then head up when ready!

For both tacks and gybes the first part of the movement tends to be slightly slower and smooth, so use the boat speed that you have, followed by a transition where the

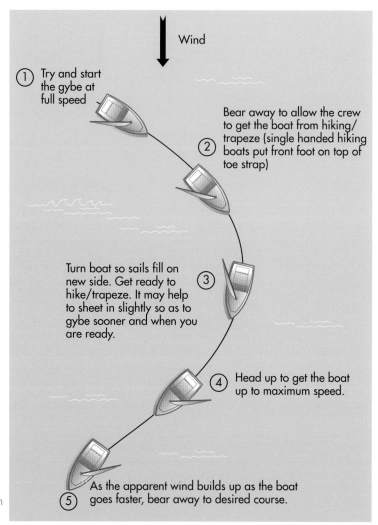

Wind

1 Try and start the gybe at full speed

2 Bear away to allow the crew to get the boat from hiking/ trapeze (single handed hiking boats put front foot on top of toe strap)

3 Turn boat so sails fill on new side. Get ready to hike/trapeze. It may help to sheet in slightly so as to gybe sooner and when you are ready.

4 Head up to get the boat up to maximum speed.

5 As the apparent wind builds up as the boat goes faster, bear away to desired course.

6.2b
Best course to sail when gybing.

boat changes direction and is brought back up to maximum speed a.s.a.p. In a tack this point is head to wind; in a gybe you need to start moving as soon as the main crosses the boat. In both tacks and gybes you need to get your weight out as soon as the sails fill, even if you subsequently move the weight back in again.

Remember, the boat speed is determined by the position of the hull, sails and crew. Whether you are hiking off just one leg, still have the tiller in the wrong hand or are not clipped onto the trapeze is irrelevant. Concentrate on maintaining speed/getting the boat back up to speed as soon as possible. Sort out the 'niceties' later (much like getting off the start line).

Exercise 1:

Have two boats line up upwind on converging tacks: one on port and one on starboard like a 'rabbit' start. The starboard boat ducks the port boat; both boats sail for three boat lengths (vary according to class and wind strength – decrease time for slower boats and weaker winds) and then tack. When they come back together, both boats tack out again, sail for three boat lengths and then tack back. Continue until one boat is clearly ahead (can cross by two boat lengths). Now review the technique.

Exercise 2:

Start on a reach. On the count of three, sheet in and then tack round, bear away and then bear away onto a dead run. Now gybe (run to run) every 30 seconds (vary according to class and wind strength – increase time for faster boats and stronger winds). Continue for 20 gybes, but stop if a boat capsizes!

Exercise 3:

Set up a slalom course. If you do not have a coach, try and find an area of moorings (without boats attached). Try sailing 120 degrees from the wind, and gybing through 120 degrees. Where possible, do at least 10 gybes in a row. The closer together the marks are, the harder the exercise is. Try to do a racing turn (in wide, out tight) as well as doing a good gybe!

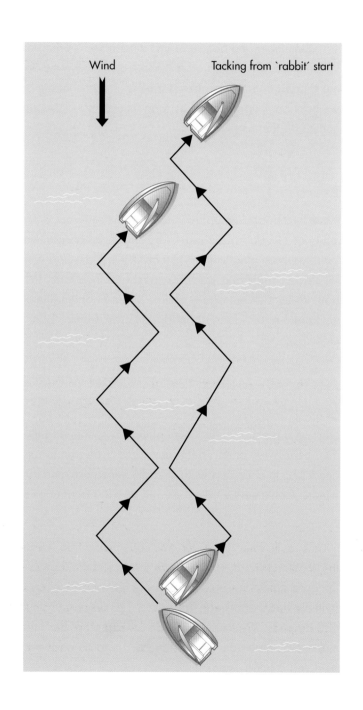

Wind

Tacking from `rabbit´ start

6.2c Exercise 1: Tacking from a 'rabbit' start.

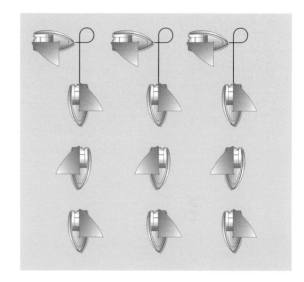

6.2d
Exercise 2: Gybing every 30 seconds.

Exercise 4:

You pretend you are sailing up a narrow river. This needs three points (ideally a coach boat and two buoys forming a start line) to make a triangle. You must stay within the triangle; you can call water at the sides. This means that those boats that end up at the front have to tack every few boat lengths to stay in the triangle (river!)

Exercise 5:

This is a windward/leeward course, with a short start line and a turning mark in the middle, called the gut-buster. You sail upwind from the start around the turning mark, to the windward mark, then downwind around the turning mark and a hook finish through the gate. The shorter the course, the harder this is. Typically, each leg should be less than a minute to make it really hard. For boats with a spinnaker, this must be hoisted and dropped when going around the turning mark.

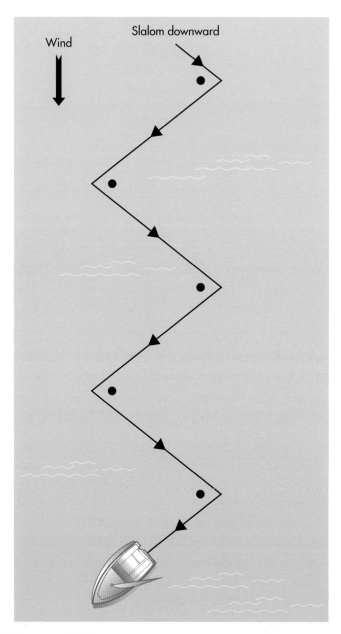

6.2e Exercise 3: Downwind slalom.

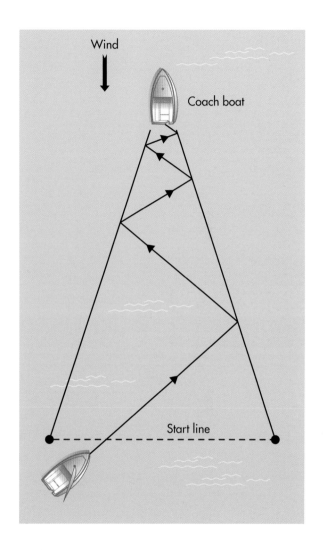

6.2f Exercise 4: Riverboat.

6.3 Changing Gear

The basic mechanics of manoeuvres are always the same when you break them right down. However, they change depending upon the conditions. While your hands and feet may be in the same place, the speed of the manoeuvre may change, or perhaps

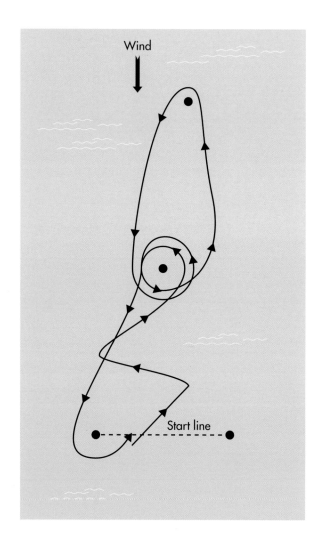

Wind

Start line

6.2g Exercise 5: Gut buster.

the amount of roll to start the turn or the amount of hiking (sitting in to stop the turn) will differ.

Wind speed	Boat handling type
Light winds	Lots of boat movement and sheeting to push the boat through the tacks and gybes. (A bit of Elvis – rock and roll!)
Medium winds	Push the boat round the corners as 'hard' as you can, and get the crew's weight from A to B as quickly as possible. (Speed is of the essence.)
Strong winds	Safety first – there will be little reward for pushing too hard. Ensure steering and crew positioning is accurate and allow extra time to do things.

If the conditions change you will not only need to change the way you manage your boat handling – which can become a lot more difficult if the breeze is fresh (force 5) to frightening (force 6 +) – but also your rig set-up. However, if it is not possible to change the rig set-up (perhaps there are some settings which can not be changed in your class during racing), you may have to adapt your boat handling to suit. Often the wind will only increase or decrease in strength for a short while, so it is not worth changing the rig from the average setting.

It is also good to try in conditions which are lighter and stronger than those you may race in. Make sure you can get back if you break something or if the wind disappears completely. In this way, when you race in the extremes of conditions it will seem easier. Remember if you only train in 8–16 knots of wind, then you will only ever be good in 8–16 knots of wind.

Boat handling is the one area where everybody is capable of doing well; it is all about practice and keeping sharp. I try to break down each manoeuvre into several sections so it is easier to analyse. For example, a leeward mark rounding would be split into entry, transition and exit. Each one of these areas can then be broken down further. It is important to master the first stage before trying to perfect the next stage, as an error early in the manoeuvre may affect the end. There is no better way to train than just repeating the manoeuvres until they are perfect. Try to be very critical when things aren't quite right, and aim for perfection. Each small gain in boat handling leads to a much bigger gain on the race course; everybody will make small mistakes, so it's all about trying to minimise these errors.

Tactics

What are Boat-to-Boat Tactics?

Upwind Tactics

Downwind Tactics

Advice from Paul Goodison

7.1 What are Boat-to-Boat Tactics?

First let us define tactics: this is the way you react to the boats around you, looking at the 'small picture'. Team racing is an area of the sport which is all about boat-to-boat tactics, because boats are directly pitted against each other and there are lots of short races. Team racing is an excellent method of improving tactical awareness. All sailors who need to improve their boat-to-boat skills are advised to do some team racing.

A good understanding of the racing rules is essential for good tactics (see Chapter 9). In fleet racing, rules are often used defensively, but in team racing they can be used very aggressively. Just knowing what your rights are in any given situation is crucial. In a tight one-on-one situation good tactics have decided medal positions on more than one occasion.

All who want to improve their tactical sailing should practise short course racing with lots of boats. This means there are many boat-to-boat situations. Training is an ideal time to do this, as you can complete more short races in a day than perhaps you would in a month of club racing.

It is also essential to have good boat handling skills, because if these are poor they may well limit your tactical options. This overview assumes that you have the required boat handling skills and appropriate rig setting for the race in question. Before you start working on your tactics, ensure that your boat handling is up to scratch (see Chapter 6).

In some races you have to beat a particular boat (perhaps in the final race of a regatta). Here your boat-to-boat tactics are vital, especially if it is a short race, and this may even affect the way you tune your boat. You should consider your tactical options at every point. Effectively this means having a mental tactical dartboard so you know what is the most important factor and how much importance or risk you can attach to it.

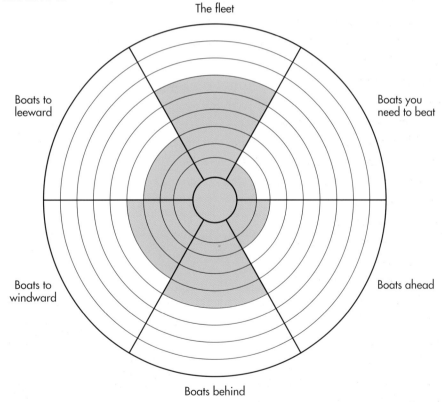

7.1 Tactical considerations dartboard.

7.2 Upwind Tactics

The most basic upwind tactic is to cover the opposition. This works most effectively when the fleet is well spread out and there are only a few boats which can attack your position. This does not work well in crowded situations. If you come out of the start leading 100 boats you can not possibly cover them all (and by concentrating on one boat you may let 99 others past!). However, on the final beat you can easily concentrate on the boat closest to you.

Cover

There are two types of cover:

- Loose cover is where you are effectively staying between the chasing boat and the next mark but not giving them too much bad air (where the wind has come off your leach before reaching their sails). This means they are likely to carry on sailing.

- Tight cover is where you are much closer and are really trying to slow the other boat down by maximising the amount of dirty air you give them. This may result in a tacking duel as the other boat tries to find clean air.

Attack and Defence

Boat-to-boat tactics is reactive sailing. That is when one boat does something to you, and you need to react immediately. You may, for example, wish (for whatever reason) to keep to the right of a boat (to get the next shift, stay in better current, etc.), so whenever it goes right, you go right.

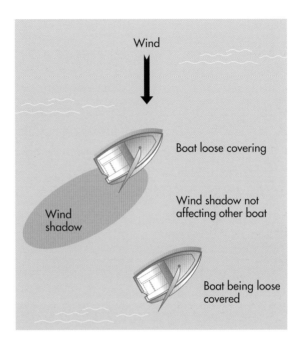

7.2a Loose covering.

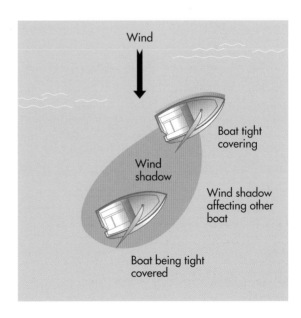

7.2b Tight covering.

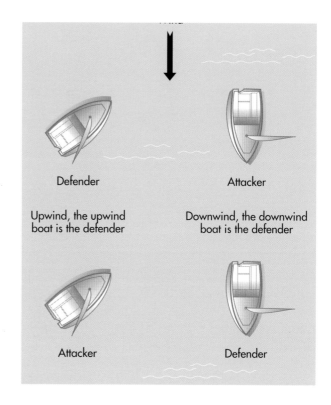

Defender

Attacker

Upwind, the upwind
boat is the defender

Downwind, the downwind
boat is the defender

Attacker

Defender

7.2c Attacker/Defender.

Remember the boat behind (whether upwind or downwind) is always the attacker. It dictates when the lead boat must tack (to cover) and can therefore force it to tack onto headers, or, when downwind, can aggressively cover the boat in front. Playing 'attacker/ defender' is a very good exercise, but it can get quite aggressive with two equally matched sailors, or quite disheartening for two mismatched sailors. It is always best to race with someone of similar abilities, ensuring that both sailors stay within the rules.

Leading the Fleet

When leading the race you must decide on your tactics to stay there: you may wish to allow the fleet to follow you.

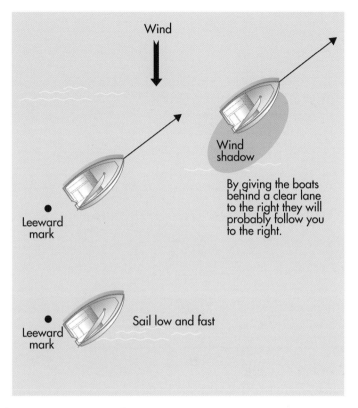

Wind

Wind
shadow

By giving the boats
behind a clear lane
to the right they will
probably follow you
to the right.

Leeward
mark

Leeward
mark

Sail low and fast

7.2d To get the fleet to go right.

To get the fleet to go right:

Sail fast and free from the leeward mark. The chasing pack will think they have rounded on a better heading and be tempted to follow you.

To get the fleet to go left:

Immediately after rounding the mark, put in a tack, then tack back, so as to give lots of dirt to the next boat. Try and cover the fleet tightly on port (giving them lots of dirt), but only cover loosely on starboard. Every time they try and go right, return to hard cover and hope they get the hint!

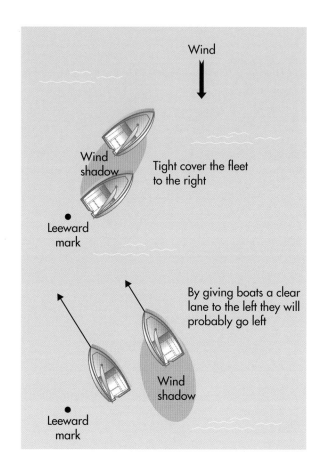

7.2e To get fhe fleet to go left.

Slowing Someone Down

Tight cover them and tack every time they tack to keep them in as much dirty air as possible. (You need to be confident that your boat handling is at least as good, but preferably better than the closest boats). Keep as close as you dare! Each tack should lose them some ground (but will also lose you some ground). It rarely pays to cover someone tightly at the beginning of a race or regatta, as you will end up giving away too much ground to other boats.

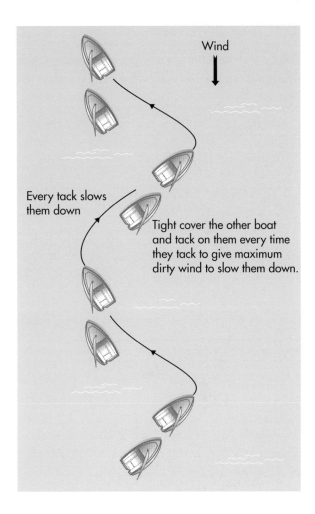

Wind

Every tack slows
them down

Tight cover the other boat
and tack on them every time
they tack to give maximum
dirty wind to slow them down.

7.2f Slowing someone down.

Consistency

If you can, try and work more towards the side of the course you believe favoured, but
stay between the fleet and the next mark of the course. If possible, try not to hit the lay
lines too early (as this will limit your options).

Sail Your Own Race

If the conditions are very flukey, you may just have to get on with your own race. The wind may be very different just 20 yards away, and you could end up losing by

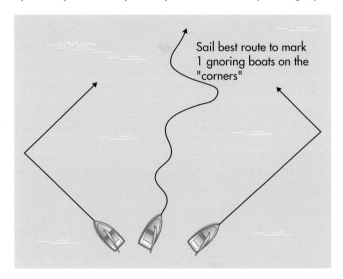

Sail best route to mark 1 gnoring boats on the "corners"

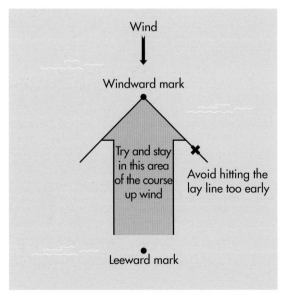

Wind

Windward mark

Try and stay in this area of the course up wind

Avoid hitting the lay line too early

Leeward mark

7.2g Sailing consistently.

trying to cover. However, if you are the fastest person in the fleet and winning, there is usually no reason for sailing your own race. You should apply at least a loose cover to the fleet, as there is no difference in the scoring between winning by an inch or by a mile.

When approaching the windward mark, make sure you do not allow room for other boats to tack inside you. You should be approaching the mark at full speed. Let the sail controls off at the last minute

When rounding marks it is important to avoid sailing through the fleet and the dirty wind and water around them. At the windward mark try and pick a side to approach from when 4–6 boat lengths away (so you are not doing lots of tacks just below the windward mark). After rounding the downwind mark/gate try to avoid tacking into the boats still coming downwind.

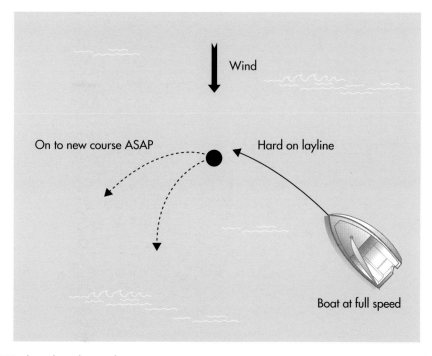

7.2h Windward mark rounding.

7.3 Downwind Tactics

Downwind, your tactics as the lead boat are usually heavily dictated by the boat behind you. Often it is simpler to try and keep your air clean and sail as fast as you can! Where possible, encourage those boats around you to work with you to get away

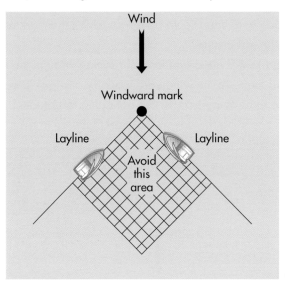

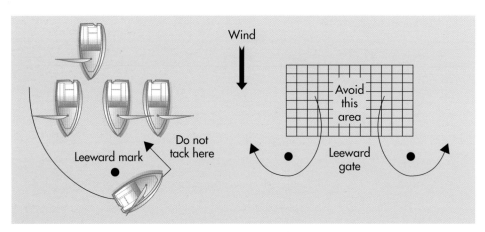

7.3a When rounding marks avoid sailing through the fleet.

from the fleet. Try and avoid getting caught in silly luffing battles (as you may end up sailing back to the windward mark), unless you are trying to slow the other boat down (and are not worried about slowing yourself down).

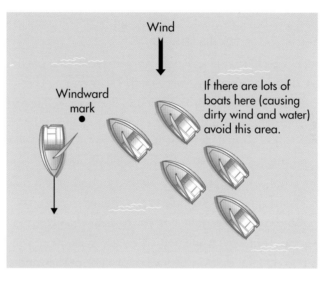

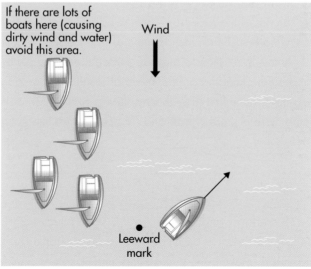

7.3a (continued)

Often the best opportunity to overtake comes at a mark, where you can possibly gain water or slow down and capitalise on someone else's bad mark rounding. As the attacker you always need to think about whether you are going to overtake to windward or leeward. Remember, in an effort to stay in front, the defending boat may well end up slowing you both down. As a defending boat you want to keep your wind clean and also stay in phase with the shifts.

Tactics for each leg of the course should be decided on the previous leg (although you are, of course, allowed to change your mind). This way you know if you are going to attack or defend your position prior to getting to the mark. If there are lots of boats just in front and a gap behind, you should be attacking, going as fast as you can. If the situation is the other way round, with boats close behind and not many places to be gained, a more conservative approach may be required. Also, on races of more than one lap, remember what you did (whether it worked or not) on the previous round. For example, did it work just staying to the right of the group?

You need to attend as many regattas as you possibly can so as to learn from real racing experience. That way, when you encounter a situation, you instinctively know how to react: to go high or low downwind, or duck or tack underneath the approaching boat on starboard tack upwind.

It is far harder to control the race from downwind as the sailors behind you will always get the new wind first! Being fast downwind (see Chapters 12 and 13) can turn you into a tactical genius. In relation to a group of boats you can always place yourself in the best tactical position: keeping on the inside of a shift; being on the side of the run which is getting the breeze first (this corresponds to going high or low on the reach depending on where there is more wind); and, of course, (just like upwind) keeping your air clean!

Exercise:

The best way to work on downwind tactics is over a small course. Start upwind for approximately the time you want to do downwind exercises (for a two-hour exercise, sail upwind for two hours, making the total sailing time approximately four hours) and have a downwind start. This is a follow-my-leader with everyone on a reach, tacking

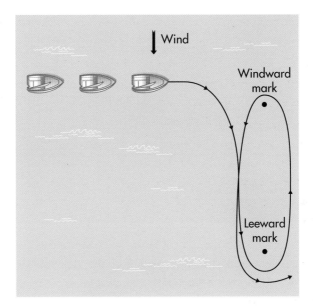

7.3b Downwind exercise.

round and bearing away together to head straight downwind. The boats then go round the leeward mark, back up to the windward mark and downwind to finish at the leeward mark.

After the Windward Mark

Downwind tactics are all about beating the boats around you, putting any extra distance in the bag. When you get around the windward mark this is not the time to relax. You need to consider what your best options are; your positioning in relation to other boats makes a real difference.

You have three options:

- Try and overtake to windward; do not go too close, as you need to keep clear. This means you may well be covering the boat in front. This works

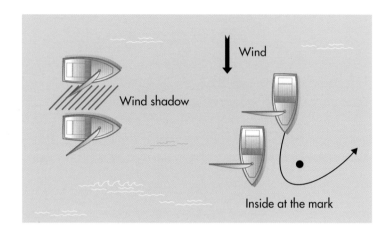

Wind

Wind shadow

Inside at the mark

7.3c Establishing an overlap to windward.

well if the next mark is being rounded on the tack you are on, as you will have the inside overlap (remember this has to be established at two boat lengths). This manoeuvre tends to work well when you can overtake quickly.

- Simply by sailing fast and going straight to the mark you can get past boats. Downwind they will often move out of your way to get clean wind. On a reach, when trying to get away from the chasing pack, this can also be the easiest way to get those boats around you to sail fast and not slow each other down.

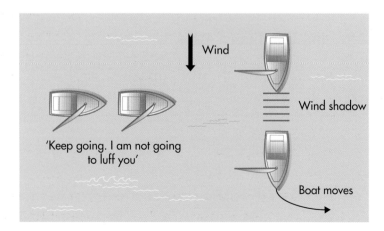

Wind

'Keep going. I am not going to luff you'

Wind shadow

Boat moves

7.3d Going straight for the mark.

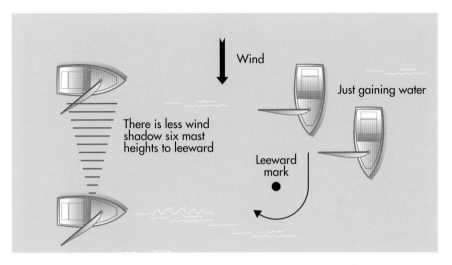

Wind

Just gaining water

There is less wind shadow six mast heights to leeward

Leeward mark

7.3e Going Low.

- Going low can give you the inside overlap at a mark if this is all you need to do to overtake. This works well if you have a small speed advantage and can go the same speed as the boat in front, but slightly lower. If you are going to break through the wind shadow you need a bit of separation.

As the defending boat your options are to try and sail fast and keep your wind free. Often a sharp luff will be enough to deter the boat behind from fighting with you. A long slow luff can see both boats sailing lots of extra distance, while losing out to boats not involved who may simply sail underneath (it may be worth trying to point this out). Often it is a case of perception. As a boat heads up, it temporarily goes faster and therefore believes it can sail over the boat in front, but when it bears away it will be the same speed as the boat in front.

Of course, as the boat in front, the best thing to do is just sail real fast so you do not have to worry about other boats. If only it was as easy as that! Some classes of boats react better or worse to dirty wind (this may vary with wind speed), so here you have to manage the potential risk by seeing which is the greater loss. You may,

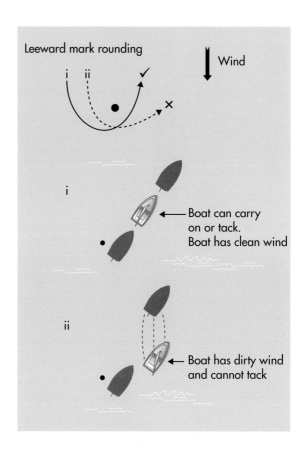

7.3f Good leeward mark rounding
(in wide, out tight).

for example, let someone sail over you and lose a boat length, but still be able to sail straight to the mark and keep your race strategy (see Chapter 8), thus gaining several boat lengths on all the boats who went high.

A good leeward mark rounding is essential so you have clean wind for the upwind leg and the option to tack. (If you sag to leeward you will be in the dirty air of the boats in front and may have no option to tack if there are boats close behind.) This is achieved by getting the sail controls sorted and entering the mark wide, so you can squeeze up tight as you exit. Remember, if there was a photo taken a boat length upwind, they should not be able to tell from the picture that you had just rounded a mark. When training, always try and finish on a leeward mark rounding, as this is one of the most difficult and important manoeuvres.

Key tactical ideas

- Clean air – keep your wind clean or get into clean wind as soon as possible.

- Stay between the opposition and the next mark (directly upwind on the upwind legs, slightly offset on the downwind legs) so as to have clean wind.

- Protect the favoured side of the course (the side with more wind, better current, etc.)

Advice from Paul Goodison:

I feel the key to tactics is being able to adapt quickly to changing situations. It is very much about weighing up the risk/reward for each action on the race course. Try and minimise risks and sail conservatively. Generally, the people who make the fewest mistakes win. It is important to be able to focus on the right thing at the right time. Different weather conditions and fleet positions will require different tactics. I try and keep things as simple as possible, and set myself small goals for different conditions. For example, in shifty conditions I will always be on the lifted tack, sometimes even if this means I am in dirty air. In stable conditions, I always make sure that I have clear wind. This may mean I have to take a small header to clear my lane. I set out these goals for each day, as they are dependent on the conditions and stage of the regatta. It is easy to overcomplicate this area of sailing: generally the people that are winning are just keeping it simple.

Strategy

What is Strategy?

Upwind Strategy

Downwind Strategy

Advice from Simon Hiscocks

8.1 What is Strategy?

Strategy is the way you would sail around a course as quickly as possible if there were no other boats present (always with a clear wind, never having to keep clear of anyone, etc.). Good race strategy is the way you would sail when leading a handicap race where you were the fastest boat, as opposed to sailing in a tight one-design class where you were just in the lead.

At some venues the strategy may be very obvious, as there will be clear patterns in the wind or the current, for example, but at others it will not. It is often very hard to coach yourself in strategy, as you will often find yourself in unexpected scenarios (light winds at a 'strong wind venue', for example). If the wind really increases, the waves have more effect than the current. In a wind against tide scenario upwind it may then pay to be in flatter water rather than the more favourable current. It may also pay to be in the bigger waves downwind.

In order to look at strategy it is good to train on your own, or perhaps with a single training partner (of similar speed).

By practising at a venue well before an event, in the absence of other boats, you can see how (in an 'ideal' world) you would sail around a race course in different winds and currents.

Strategy will vary a lot from class to class and depend upon the wind's strength. For example, in marginal planing conditions (for a particular class) wind speed may be the most important factor. On a shifty day, being on the right tack may be the most important thing. However, if the wind speed and current speed are similar, current will be the deciding factor if there is a difference in water flow across the race course (especially for the slower boats or those which lose a lot of speed tacking).

Getting out on the race course early on race day, and training at the venue as much as possible before an important event are highly recommended. This will give you a good idea of the wind, waves and current to expect at different areas of the course. Find someone of similar speed to yourself and do split tacks. You both set off from the middle of the line on different tacks, and after an agreed time (say five minutes) you both tack back. See who is in front when you meet, and most importantly, why!

Tide is often a huge factor in deciding race strategy. Unlike the wind, current can be accurately predicted! Race strategy often starts many hours, weeks, months or even years before the first race! Do your homework by looking at tidal and meteorological data beforehand.

The best way of approaching a race is to decide the main strategy, for there may be several strategies in conflict. For example, one side of the course may have more adverse tide but also more wind. Sailing is a very dynamic sport: there are often many variables. When you have all the available information, you can make an informed decision. We will now consider several factors, one at time (assuming that no other factors are applicable). You will notice there is often a link between the upwind and downwind strategy, so when thinking ahead always consider what is currently paying and more importantly WHY.

On any particular race day there will be factors that are the most important. For slow boats, current may make the most difference. For faster boats in light winds it may be finding the areas of the course with the most wind. For boats which tack and gybe easily and are at near maximum hull speed, it will be all about the shifts.

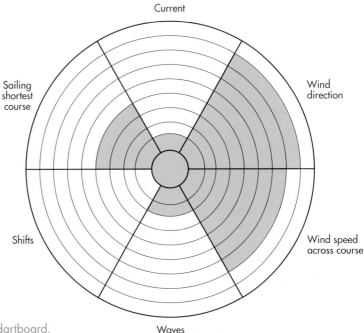

8.1
Strategic considerations dartboard.

8.2 Upwind Strategy

If the current is flowing in more or less the same direction as the windward mark, it obviously pays to sail towards the area of maximum flow when beating. But be careful not to overstand the top mark.

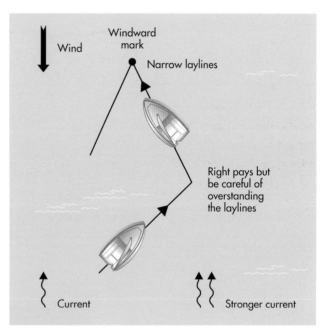

8.2a Current under the fleet.

If the current is in the same direction as the wind, you want to stay out of the strong current for as long as possible. Remember that the lay lines will be broader. When the current is against you, your top priority may well be to get out of the tide. It may even pay to slightly overstand the marks.

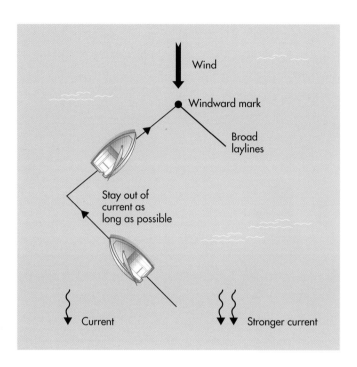

8.2b Current against fleet.

If the current is across the course upwind there should be no difference, but once

again pay careful attention to the lay lines. You want to do the long tack first as it keeps you towards the centre of the course and thus keeps your options open. Tidal flows can change considerably during a day. Always get accurate data, and if possible drop a tide stick (a bottle half full of water will do) near the marks of the course to see what the current is doing.

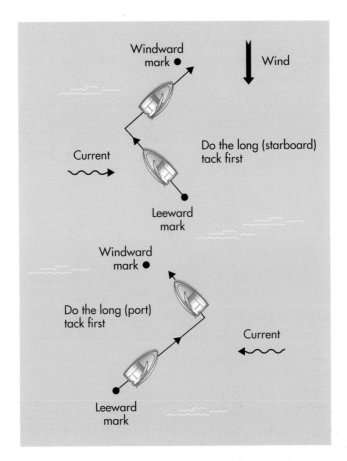

Windward
mark ●

Wind

Do the long (starboard)
tack first

Current

Leeward
mark

Windward
mark ●

Do the long (port)
tack first

Current

Leeward
mark

8.2c
Current across the course.

In the absence of tide, we may simply be considering the wind. If the wind
is oscillating, we need to stick towards the centre of the course, so we can take
advantage of as many wind shifts as possible, tacking on headers upwind. Upwind we
are going towards the wind and going slower, so there will tend to be more shifts to

take advantage of (tack for). Also, if we are approaching a shore, the frequency of the shifts may increase as we go upwind.

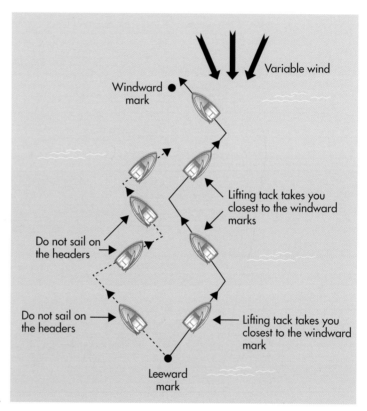

Windward mark

Variable wind

Lifting tack takes you closest to the windward marks

Do not sail on the headers

Do not sail on the headers

Lifting tack takes you closest to the windward mark

Leeward mark

8.2d Tacking on the shifts.

The more ground lost by tacking, the bigger the shift needs to be before it is worth tacking on. Remember, if the breeze is shifty you want to head towards the centre of the course so that you always have the option to tack in the shifts. If there are lots of lifts on one tack, you want to be sailing on the other tack when the wind returns to its mean wind direction. (If, for example, the windward leg is quite short, then on each beat the breeze will predominantly be shifting one way.)

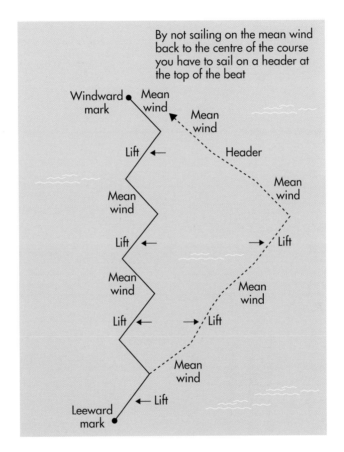

By not sailing on the mean wind back to the centre of the course you have to sail on a header at the top of the beat

8.2e
Staying towards the centre of the course.

If the land is parallel to the race course and on the left, as the wind backs over the land there will be an area of convergence near the shore. This means there will be more wind on the left. If there is a headland, the wind tends to funnel around this, once again meaning that there will be more wind near the end of the headland. More wind can make a real difference to upwind boat speed.

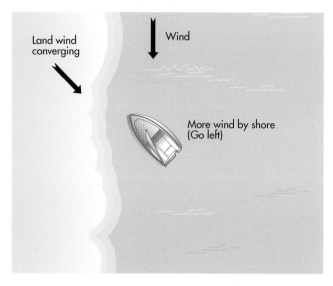

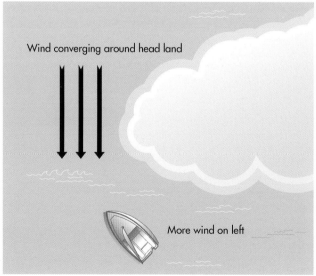

8.2f
Sailing for the pressure.

If there is a wind bend, it may be caused by a landmass, which will dictate the favoured side. Here, you need to be very careful not to tack too early and miss the centre of the wind bend, but remember you may need to tack under the expected lay line, as you will be lifted out on the other tack.

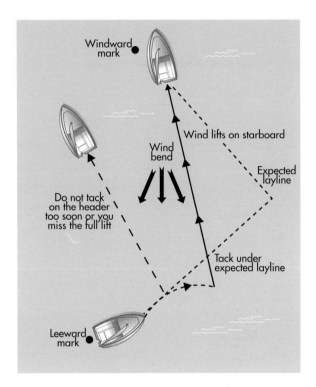

8.2g Wind bend, sail toward the centre of the wind bend before tacking.

There may be an expected shift because of the formation of a sea breeze, or perhaps the weather forecast has predicted a change of wind direction. Often you can spot the change of breeze by looking at smoke coming off the land, flags on shore or other boats upwind. Here, you want to get yourself to the required side before the shift occurs, so as to be able to take full advantage of it (but once again remembering lay lines).

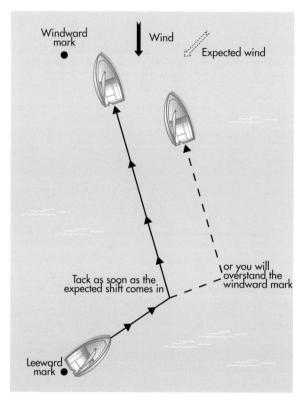

8.2h
Expected shift (being on the right side).

The expected shift may not happen all at once: there may be a gradual shift with the breeze turning 10 degrees or so every hour. In this case, you always want to be moving towards the way the wind is turning when you are not on a lift.

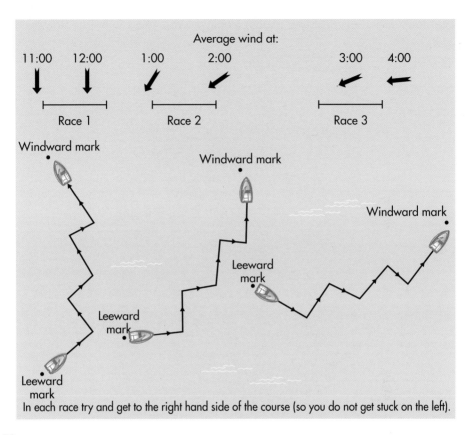

8.2i
Sailing with a persistent shift.

Water friction causes the formation of waves, which can have a profound effect on boat speed. Basically, if you are going over the waves (sailing upwind in a nonplaning boat or planing over waves), you wish to find the flattest area of the race course, as this may have a bigger effect than, for example, the current. On a smaller (tactical) scale, you may simply be looking for a flatter spot to put a tack in. It may be worth sailing a boat length over the lay line if it means you can do a decent tack. Wind against tide produces big waves; wind with tide flattens the water.

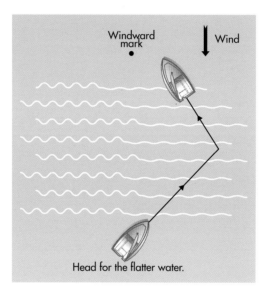

8.2j
Looking to avoid the waves.

A consistent approach tends to win regattas, so it may well be wise to choose to play the percentages and follow your strategy 70%, but not go the whole hog, in case you are mistaken. An all or nothing approach may win a race or even an open, but will rarely, if ever, win a championship. Sailing is a sport where the race is not over until it is over. Until you cross the finish line you are never sure of your position (and even then it can change as a result of protest!). Watch the fleet and remember that you get exactly the same number of points whether you win a race by an inch or a mile!

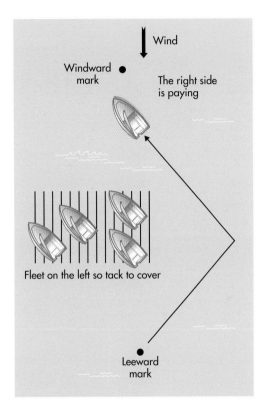

8.2k
Playing the percentages.

8.3 Downwind Strategy

On a reach you are usually just using the current flow to help you minimise the distance sailed. The quickest route on a reach is a straight line (as it is the shortest distance), so the course sailed should reflect the current flow. This assumes the wind strength remains constant, and that by going high or low you would not find an area of less wind.

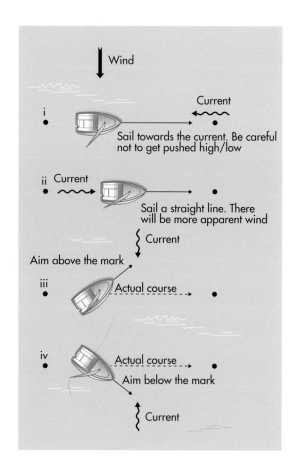

8.3a
Using the current to sail a straight line on the reach.

On the run it will also pay to be towards the side of maximum flow, but weighing it against sailing the extra distance.

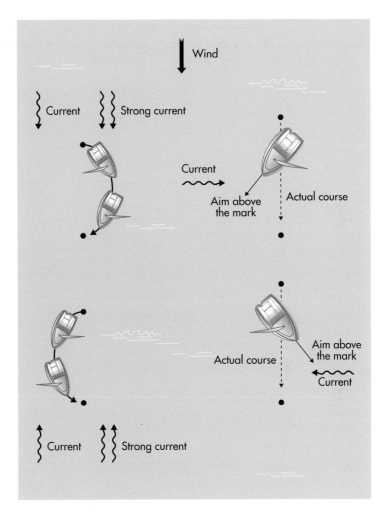

Wind

Current   Strong current

Current

Aim above
the mark

Actual course

Actual course

Aim above
the mark

Current

Current   Strong current

8.3b
Choosing the favoured side of the run for current.

Downwind you need to gybe to sail on the headers (the favoured tack) just as upwind you tack to sail on the lifts (the favoured tack). Therefore you gybe on the lifts downwind, just as you tack on the headers upwind. This means you sail the shortest distance to the next mark. However, in boats with unstayed rigs you may choose to sail by the lee. In this case, you will be sailing on the opposite tack, with the airflow going the other way (from leach to luff) across the sail.

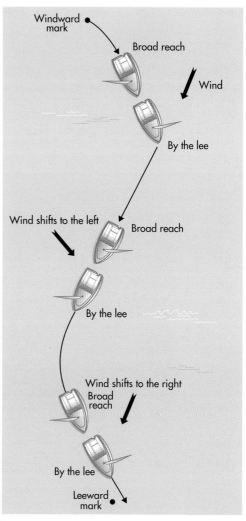

8.3c
Gybing on the shifts.

Downwind pressure is very important. Always try and position yourself so you are lined up for the wind. The faster the boat, the more the wind approaches from the side.

For example, in an Optimist, the wind will be directly from behind, while for a Tornado travelling at speed the wind will be coming much more from the side. You need to stay in the pressure for as long as possible, but take the opportunity to move back towards the centre of the course (unless all the boats are on the same side as you) to put the gains made in the bank.

If the land is parallel to the race course, then there will be more wind on one side of the race course due to convergence/divergence (see Chapter 3). When looking upwind, if the land is on the right, then there will be more wind on the offshore side of

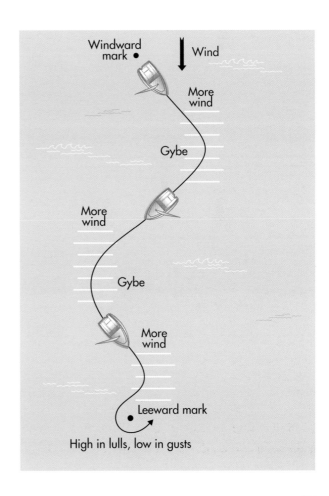

8.3d
Centre of course.

the race course; if the land is on your left then there will be more wind on the inshore side of the race course. Pressure tends to come down the course in patches. By bearing away in the gusts it is possible to stay in them for longer, and this also enables you to head up in the lulls to maintain your average boat speed. When sailing downwind you steer less, so pressure is king. You may need to gybe to stay in pressure. When you get the opportunity, move to sail a conservative race, but remember an extra knot or two of breeze can make a real difference.

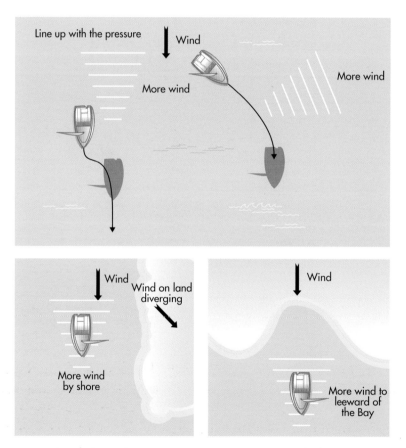

8.3e
Pressure differences across the course.

The local topography may mean that one side of the course has more pressure than the other: this side is then favoured both up and downwind. A good example of this would be Lake Garda.

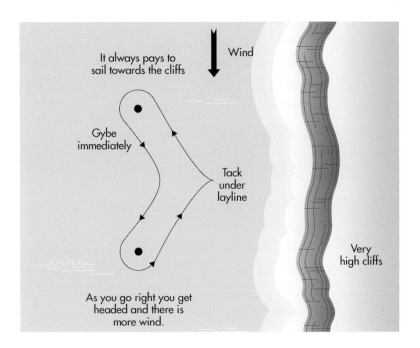

8.3f
Head for the cliffs at Garda.

Waves can make a real difference downwind. If you are surfing, you want to find the best ride, and this means the biggest waves (both in terms of height and length) you can catch! Whereas in light winds you do not want the waves to slow you down, in strong winds, when you can just go over them, you are looking for short wave height. This, of course, varies from boat to boat, as some boats are able to overtake the waves sooner than others.

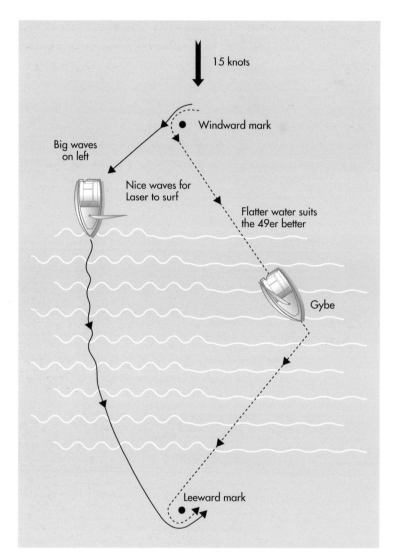

15 knots

Windward mark

Big waves
on left

Nice waves for
Laser to surf

Flatter water suits
the 49er better

Gybe

Leeward mark

8.3g
Choosing the side of the course for the waves.

Often there will be a conflict of interest: Do you bear away in the gust? Or do you continue to sail high, so as to get out of the adverse current quicker? Do you catch every wave? Or is it best to work hard to one side of the race course? Often you only know the correct answers after the race, and perhaps this is why sailing rewards those with lots of regatta experience, as they are able to recognise situations they have been in before and react instinctively. The key would be to put an old man's experience in a young man's body, hence the need for coaches!

Sometimes, the safe option may be to go to one side of the race course when the wind is gradually turning that way. (For example, in a sea breeze from 200 degrees heading towards 240, it would pay for you to protect the right-hand side of the race course, being aware of lay lines). However, you do need to be aware that

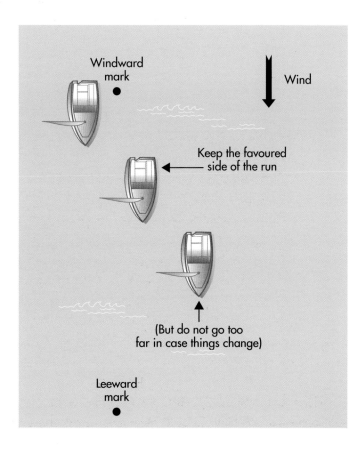

Windward mark

Wind

Keep the favoured side of the run

(But do not go too far in case things change)

Leeward mark

8.3h
Playing it safe.

the course may appear to be skewed, with the beat becoming one sided and the run approaching a broad reach. Alternatively, the marks may be moved – so 'keep your head out of the boat'!

The classic banana shape of the fleet behind the leader often explains why the leader ends up so far in front, having sailed much less distance than the chasing boats as they all try and sail a little bit above each other. Often, when seen from outside a racing boat, the shape is quite hard to believe (just the opposite of the mid-line sag often seen on the start line). If possible, find a transit so you know you are going in a straight line, allowing for any current. Remember, because you are usually steering from the windward side of the boat, the mark will look to windward of the bow.

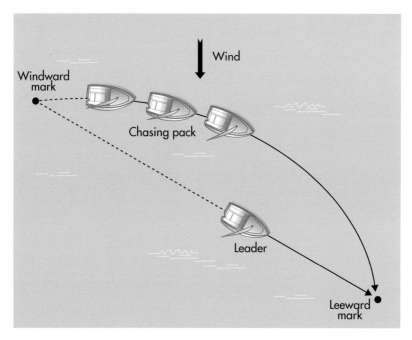

8.3i
Sailing the shortest course.

Advice from Simon Hiscocks:

Strategy is all about having a plan for how, given the opportunity, you would like to sail a race: which side of the race course you would like to go to or to protect.

A lot of strategy can be done before going on the water. Local topography will affect the wind and tides and can be checked out with a chart and tide table. There may even be a fair amount of public information regarding racing on the course areas at popular venues. Asking people who have raced at the venue beforehand or locals might reveal a lot of local knowledge, which, combined with the rules on wind bends, convergence and divergence, will cover most of the course scenarios.

Once on the water, try to work out what type of day it is. Is it gusty or steady? How large are the wind shifts and how fast are they? All these factors affect a number of rules that you might create for the day, or for a particular race. Be careful of making too many rules – or at least be open minded about the rules, so they can be changed if they don't appear to be working! Adding this information to some of the defined factors, such as start line or course bias and any venue knowledge, will help to form a plan. It doesn't have to be a very defined plan; it can be pretty broad. For instance, it might be to start mid line and go with the shift at the time, simply because you cannot create anything more substantial. You now know where you want to start and you know what information you are looking for. Once started there are only two options to take. It defines how the team will work and how the tactical decisions will be made.

Rules

Rules: the Basics

Using the Rules Aggressively

Using the Rules Defensively

Advice from Simon Hiscocks

9.1   Rules: the Basics

This book has only a single chapter about rules, but it is strongly recommended that you really get into detail and learn them. After all, you need to know the rules before you can obey them – and even use them to your advantage. However, this chapter will certainly give you the basics.

Before you even get on the race course you should know the rules, as a nasty collision could result if you don't. A rule book is part of your essential kit for any regatta and a vital part of your race preparation. Every four years (each Olympic cycle) some small changes are made, so take care to keep up with these. Remember, the rules are slightly different for different areas of the sport: fleet, match and team racing.

However, the fundamentals remain the same, in line with the principles of sportsmanship: if you break a rule you will promptly take a penalty, which may be to retire from the race. Failure to obey the rules may see you severely penalised. You must use the wind and the water to increase, maintain or decrease your boat's speed. You may adjust the trim of the sails and the hull, and perform other acts of seamanship, but must not otherwise use your body to propel the boat, other than to exaggerate the roll in a tack or gybe (as long as the speed coming out of the tack or gybe is not greater than going in) and to prompt surfing or planing, when you are allowed one pump per wave or gust.

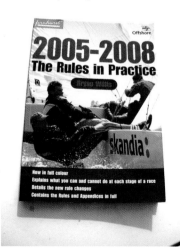

Definitions

Understanding the definitions is essential:

Abandon: A race that a race committee or protest committee abandons is void but may be resailed.

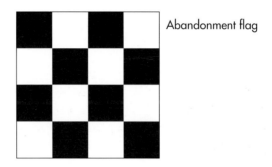

Abandonment flag

All races abandoned. Return to start area.

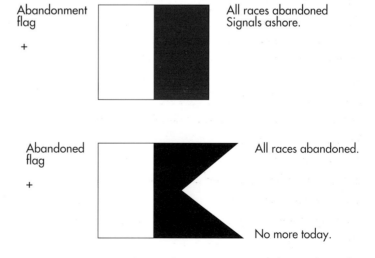

Abandonment flag

+

All races abandoned
Signals ashore.

Abandoned flag

+

All races abandoned.

No more today.

9.1a Abandonment flag.

Clear astern, clear ahead, overlap: One boat is clear astern of another when her hull and equipment in normal sailing position are behind a line abeam from the aftermost point of the other boat's hull and equipment in its normal sailing position. The other boat is clear ahead. They overlap when neither is clear astern. However, they are also overlapped when a boat between them overlaps both. These terms do not apply to boats on opposite tacks unless rule 18 applies (rounding and passing marks and obstructions).

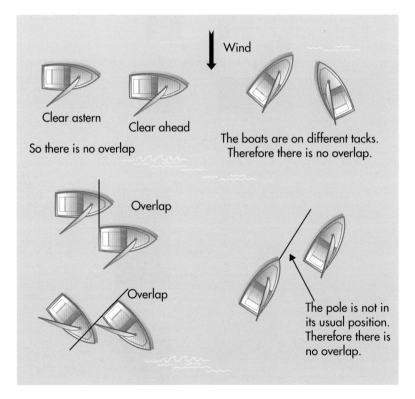

9.1b Overlap.

Finish: A boat finishes when any part of her hull, or crew, or equipment in normal position, crosses the finishing line in the direction of the course from the last mark, either for the first time, or after taking a penalty under rules 31.2 and 44.2 or under rule 28.1 after correcting an error at the finishing line.

Interested party: A person who may gain or lose as a result of a protest committee's decision, or who has a close personal interest in the decision.

Keep clear: One boat keeps clear of another if the other can sail her course with no need to take avoiding action and, when the boats are overlapped on the same tack, if the leeward boat can change course in both directions without immediately making contact with the windward boat.

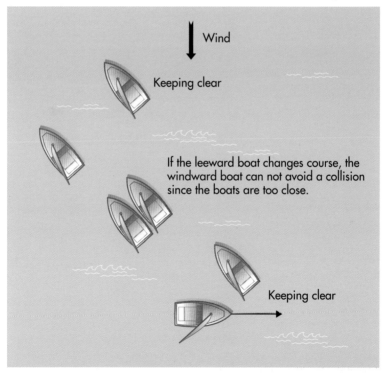

9.1c Keeping clear.

Leeward and windward: A boat's leeward side is the side that is or, when she is head to wind, was away from the wind. However, when sailing by the lee or directly downwind, her leeward side is the side on which the mainsail lies. The other side is her windward side. When two boats on the same tack overlap, the one on the leeward side of the other is the leeward boat. The other is the windward boat.

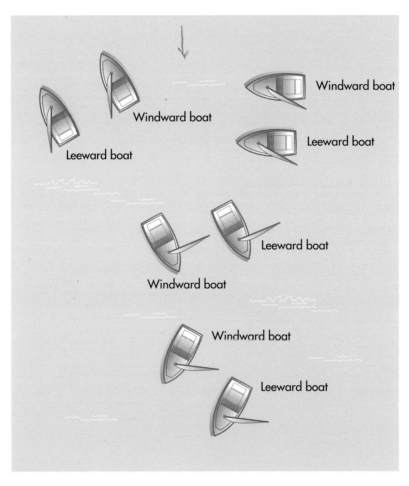

9.1d Leeward and windward.

Mark: An object which the sailing committee requires a boat to leave on a specified side, and a race committee boat surrounded by navigable water from which the starting or finishing line extends. An anchor line and objects attached temporarily or accidentally to a mark are not part of it.

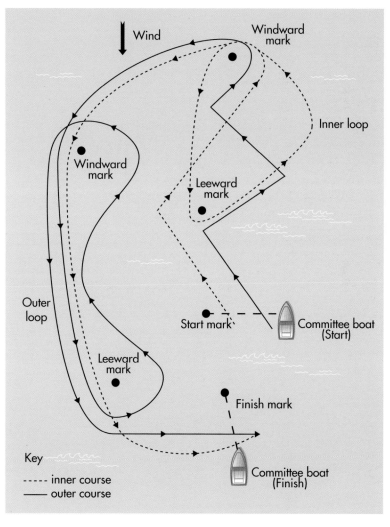

9.1e A mark.

Obstruction: An object that a boat could not pass without changing course substantially, if she were sailing directly towards it and is one of her hull lengths from it. An object that can be safely passed on only one side and an area so designated by the sailing instructions are also obstructions. However, a boat racing is not an obstruction to other boats unless they are required to keep clear of her, give her room or, if rule 21 applies, avoid her.

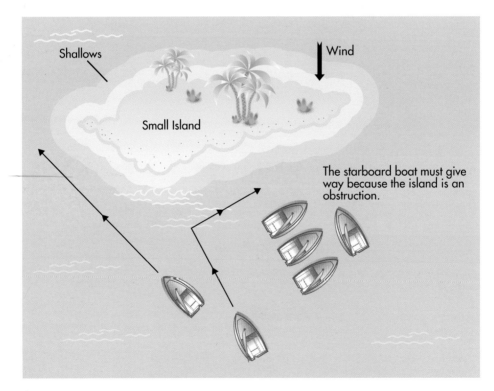

9.1f
Obstructions.

Party: A party to a hearing: a protestor; a protestee; a boat requesting redress; a boat or a competitor that may be penalised under rule 69.1; a race committee or an organizing authority in a hearing under rule 62.1 (a).

Postpone: A postponed race is delayed before its scheduled start but may be started or abandoned later.

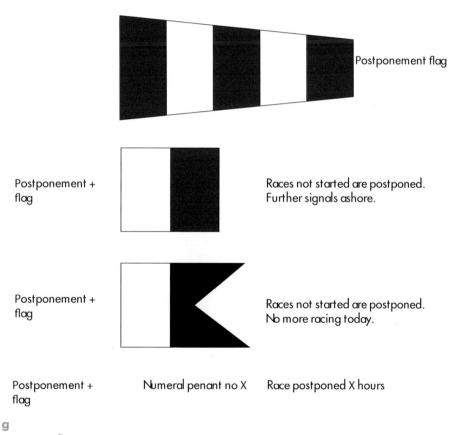

Postponement flag

Postponement + flag

Races not started are postponed. Further signals ashore.

Postponement + flag

Races not started are postponed. No more racing today.

Postponement + flag

Numeral penant no X

Race postponed X hours

9.1g
Postponement flag.

Proper course: A course a boat would sail to finish as soon as possible in the absence of the other boats referred to in the rules using the term. A boat has no proper course before the starting signal.

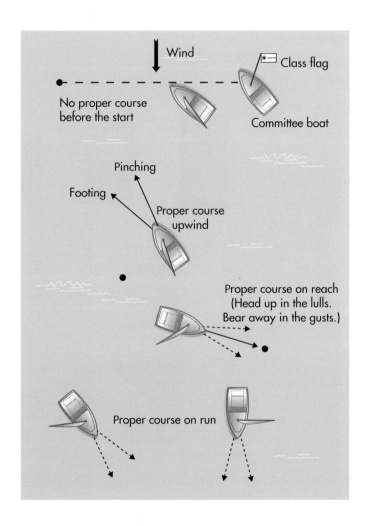

9.1h Proper course.

Protest: An allegation made under rule 61.2 by a boat, a race committee or a protest committee that a boat has broken a rule.

Protest Form – also for requests for redress and reopening

---

1. EVENT .... Organizing authority ....

Date of race.. Race number / title ....

---

2. TYPE OF HEARING: Tick as appropriate.

Protest by boat against boat ❏   Request for redress by boat or race committee ❏

Protest by race committee against boat ❏   Consideration of redress by protest committee ❏

Protest by protest committee against boat ❏ Request by boat or race committee to reopen hearing ❏

Consideration of reopening by protest committee ❏

---

3. BOAT PROTESTING, OR REQUESTING REDRESS OR REOPENING

Boat name .... Class .... Sail number ....

Represented by .... Member of ....

Address ....

.... Post code .... Tel ....

---

4. BOAT(S) PROTESTED OR BEING CONSIDERED FOR REDRESS

Boat name .... Class .... Sail number ....

---

5. INCIDENT

Time and place of incident .... Rule(s) alleged to have been broken ....

Names of witness(es) ....

---

6. INFORMING PROTESTEE. How did you inform the protestee of your intention to protest?

By hailing ❏   When? .... Word(s) used...............

By displaying a red flag ❏   When? ....

By informing her in some other way ❏   When and where? ....

PROTESTOR'S DIAGRAM	PROTESTER'S DESCRIPTION OF INCIDENT
One square = one boat length **Show on diagram:** Wind direction and strength Current direction and strength Mark, and direction to next mark Position of boats—before, during and after incident	

9.1i

Protest form.

THIS SIDE FOR RACE OFFICE AND PROTEST COMMITTEE USE:

❏ Withdrawal requested by party, signed ....

❏ Withdrawal permitted by protest committee

Hearing number [   ]

Heard together with number(s) ....

Protest time limit .... hr .... min.   Protest received [by ....] [by Race Office] at .... hr .... min.

Protest is: - in time ❏   - out of time, hearing is closed ❏   - out of time, but limit extended for good reason stated in 'Facts Found' ❏

All parties represented at the hearing ❏   or: The following party .... was notified of the time and

place of the hearing, but did not come to the hearing: the Protest Committee decided to proceed with the hearing ❏

Protestor / party requesting redress or reopening represented by ....

Protestee / boat being considered for redress / race committee represented by ....

Remarks

Objection about interested party	❏	....
Written protest or request identifies incident	❏	....
'Protest' hailed at first reasonable opportunity	❏	....
No hail needed, protestee informed at first reasonable opportunity	❏	....
Red flag conspicuously displayed at first reasonable opportunity	❏	....
Red flag seen by race committee at finish	❏	....
Red flag not needed	❏	....

Protest or request valid, hearing will continue ❏   Date of hearing .... Protest or request invalid, hearing is closed ❏

Witnesses (name / boat number) .... Interpreter ....

FACTS FOUND

....
....
....
....
....
....
....
....
....
....

Diagram of boat .... is endorsed by the committee ❏   Committee's diagram is attached ❏   No committee diagram unless requested ❏

CONCLUSIONS AND RULES THAT APPLY

....
....
....
....
....
....

DECISION

Protest is: - Dismissed ❏   - Upheld ❏   In race number .... boat .... is: Disqualified ❏   Penalized as follows ❏

....

Request for redress is: - Refused ❏   - Granted ❏ : The following redress is awarded

....

Request to reopen hearing is: - Refused ❏   - Granted ❏   Hearing to be reopened now / at ....

Protest Committee chaired by .... Signed .... Date & time ....

Other Protest Committee members ....

Written decision requested by: - Protestor ❏   - Protestee ❏   Date transmitted ....

9.1i
(Continued)

Racing: A boat is racing from her preparatory signal until she finishes and clears the finishing line and marks or retires, or until the race committee signals a general recall, postponement or abandonment.

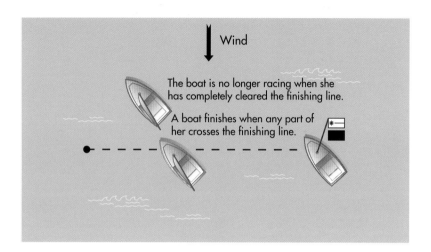

9.1j
Boat finishing.

Room: The space a boat needs in the existing conditions while manoeuvring promptly in a seamanlike way.

Rule:

(a) The current racing rules of sailing including the Definitions, Race signals, Introduction, preambles and the rules of relevant appendices, but not titles;

(b) ISAF regulation 19, Eligibility Code; Regulation 20; Advertising code; and Regulation 21, Anti-Doping code;

(c) the prescriptions of the national authority, unless they are changed by the sailing instructions in compliance with the national authority's prescriptions, if any, to rule 87

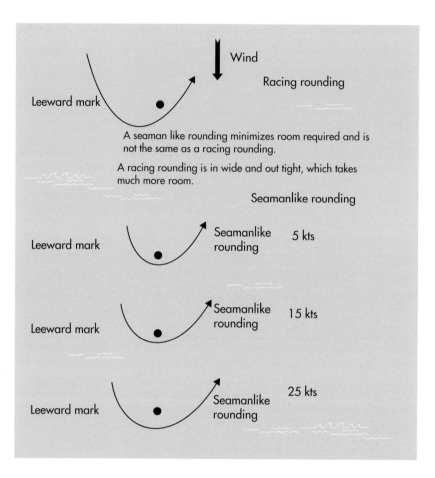

Wind

Racing rounding

Leeward mark

A seaman like rounding minimizes room required and is not the same as a racing rounding.

A racing rounding is in wide and out tight, which takes much more room.

Seamanlike rounding

Leeward mark   Seamanlike rounding   5 kts

Leeward mark   Seamanlike rounding   15 kts

Leeward mark   Seamanlike rounding   25 kts

9.1k
Room.

(d) the class rules;

(e) the notice of race;

(f) the sailing instructions and

(g) any other documents which govern the event.

STANDARD SAILING INSTRUCTIONS 2007 (Iss 07/1)
International **Laser** UK Class Association

1.   RULES

1.1   Racing will be governed by the Racing Rules of Sailing (RRS), the prescriptions of the RYA, the rules of the International Laser Class (ILCA), the International UK Laser Class Association (UKLA), these Sailing Instructions and Notice of Race. Advertising is permitted under the Advertising Code and the Laser Class is unrestricted Category C.

1.2   A copy of the .... will either be given to each competitor or displayed on the Official Notice Board at least 90 minutes before the start of the first race affected. Flag L will not be displayed.

2.   CONDITIONS OF ENTRY

2.1   The entry form requires the name of the competitor and the number of the boat. Points scored will be awarded to the competitor and no other person shall compete in that Laser in the Event. The competitor shall be a fully paid member of ILCA.

2.2.1 A competitor is entirely responsible for his/her own safety whether afloat or ashore and nothing in the Notice of Race or Sailing Instructions or anywhere else reduces this responsibility.

2.2.2 It is for the competitor to decide if he/she is fit to sail in the conditions he/she might encounter and by launching or going to sea the competitor confirms that he/she is fit for those conditions and competent to sail and compete in them.

2.2.3 The competitor is required to hold adequate insurance and in particular to hold insurance against third party claims in the sum of at least £2,000,000.

2.2.4 Nothing done by the organizers can reduce the responsibility of the competitor nor will it make the organizers responsible for any loss, damage, death, or personal injury however it may have occurred as a result of a competitor taking part in the racing. The organizers encompass everyone helping to run the race and the event, and include the organizing authority, the race committee, the race officer, safety boats and beach-masters.

2.2.5 The provision of patrol boats does not relieve the competitor of his/her responsibilities.

2.3   A Laser shall display above the waterline while racing:
(a) A sticker as supplied by UKLA denoting current class membership.
(b) Any event sponsor sticker supplied at registration, at the bow on each side of the hull. If one is lost, a replacement shall be sought on going ashore.
This SI is not protestable by another Laser & changes RRS 60.1.

2.4   The Standard fleet will race as one fleet but is sub-divided into Gold, Silver and Bronze categories as described in the Notice of Race. Standard Lasers shall display a coloured band, issued by the Race Committee, on the lower part of the mast between the deck and boom, as follows: *Gold fleet – yellow band: Silver fleet – blue band. Bronze fleet - red band.*
This can be secured either with tape or the supplied rubber bands. A Laser that loses a band shall seek a replacement on going ashore. This SI is not protestable by any other Laser. This changes RRS 60.1.

3.   SAFETY

3.1   Adequate personal buoyancy (with a minimum buoyancy of at least 50 Newtons and being either a life-jacket or a waistcoat-type buoyancy aid) shall be worn while afloat. Flag Y will not be displayed. This changes RRS 40.

3.2   The host club's .... may specify a tally system. Each time a Laser does not comply with this tally system within the time limit in the .... a non-returnable fee of £5 shall be paid to the UKLA before the UKLA races again. The penalty for non-payment will be disqualification from all races in the event.

3.3   This prevails over anything to the contrary in any local instruction or club rule. After the event, the fee will be donated to RNLI.

4.   COMMUNICATION WITH COMPETITORS

4.1   The class flags, used as warning signals, are:-
Standard - Red Laser symbol on a white background.
Radial - Red Laser symbol on a green background.
4.7   - Red Laser symbol on a yellow background

4.2   Notices to Competitors will be posted on the Official Notice Board.

4.3   Changes to these Sailing Instructions will be posted on the Official Notice Board at least 90 minutes before the first race of the day.

4.4   A whistle blown by a member of the protest committee during a race 'a member of the protest committee believes a boat has broken a rule'.

4.5   For identification purposes 'sail number' shall mean a maximum of the four last digits of a Laser sail number. If as a result there is a conflict between two or more 'sail numbers' the International Laser UK Class Association will allocate modified number(s) to be displayed by one or more of the boats throughout the event.

5.   COURSES

5.1   The diagrams are illustrative only, not to scale, and do not show the bearing or distance of any mark from any other mark. All marks to be rounded to port. The first mark of the course is mark 1.

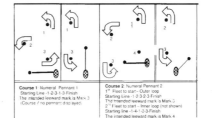

Course 1: Numeral Pennant 1
Starting Line -1-2-3-1-3-Finish
The intended leeward mark is Mark 3
(Course if no pennant displayed)

Course 2: Numeral Pennant 2
1ˢᵗ Fleet to start- Outer loop
Starting Line -1-2-3-2-3-Finish
The intended leeward mark is Mark 3
2ⁿᵈ Fleet to start - Inner loop (not shown)
Starting line -1-4-1-2-3-Finish
The intended leeward mark is Mark 4

5.2   **DESCRIPTION OF MARKS**
The starting mark, the course marks, the substitute mark (if any) and the finishing mark(s) will be described in the ....

5.3   **CHANGE OF COURSE AFTER THE START**
When it is necessary and possible, the race committee will either move the position of the mark, or lay the substitute mark.

5.4   **SHORTENING COURSE**

5.4.1 No course will be shortened until the Lasers have reached the intended leeward mark.

5.4.2 Subject to SI 5.4.1, any course may be shortened at any mark. In addition, when a finishing line described in SI 8 has been laid in the vicinity of the intended leeward mark, and when flag S is displayed with two sound signals from the finishing boat the meaning of flag S is changed to: 'The course is changed, and the intended leeward mark is the last mark of the course. Pass the mark to port and finish'.

6.   STARTS

6.1   The warning signal for the first race of the day is intended to be made at 1155 on the Saturday and at 0955 on the Sunday. It is intended that five races will be sailed in the event, target 3 on Saturday, maximum 3 on any day, back-to-back. No warning signal shall be made after 1500 hours on Sunday. When the race committee decides that a race not yet started on the Sunday cannot be completed in the time available for the event, it will signal N or H and post a cancellation notice ashore.

6.2   Races will be started using RRS 26. It is intended that the first start will be for the Standard Laser fleet, followed by the Radial fleet, followed by the 4.7 fleet, where applicable.

The warning signal for the subsequent starts will be made either with the starting signal for the previous start, or as soon as possible thereafter (without flag AP needing to be displayed).

9.11
Standard sailing instructions.

Start: A boat starts when, having been entirely on the pre-start side of the starting line at or after her starting signal, and having complied with rule 30.1 if it applies, any part of her hull, crew or equipment crosses the starting line in the direction of the first mark.

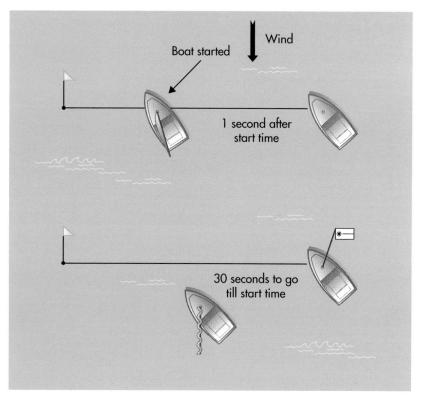

9.1m
Boat starting.

Tack (starboard or port): A boat is on a tack, starboard or port, corresponding to her windward side.

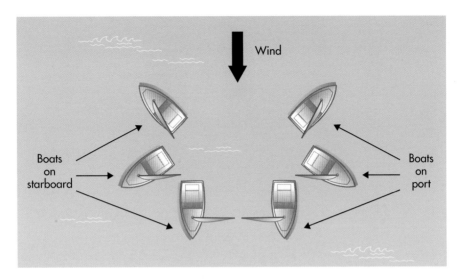

9.1n
Boats on port and starboard.

Two-length zone: The area around a mark or obstruction within a distance of two hull lengths of the boat nearer to it.

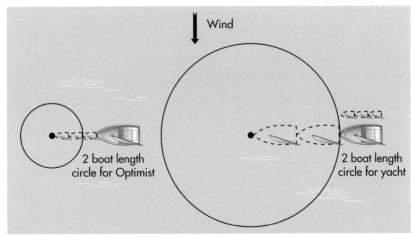

9.1o
Two–boat–length circle.

9.2   Using the Rules Aggressively

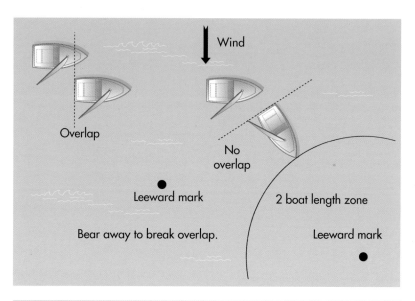

Wind

Overlap

No overlap

Leeward mark

Bear away to break overlap.

2 boat length zone

Leeward mark

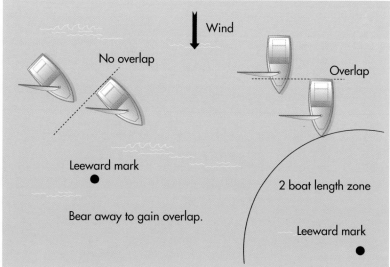

Wind

No overlap

Overlap

Leeward mark

Bear away to gain overlap.

2 boat length zone

Leeward mark

9.2a
Water at the mark.

The majority of instances occur when two boats meet, which is covered in part two of the rule book. Photocopy this section and learn it by heart.

One of the situations where places are gained is at marks, as this is where lots of boats come together. Upon entering the two-boat-length circle you need to be pointing straight towards the mark, so as to minimise the chance of their getting water on you, and maximise the chances of getting an overlap on another boat.

To get off the start line effectively a boat needs space to leeward. By completing a tack under a boat to windward (remember you must keep clear whilst tacking and must bear away to a close hauled course to complete the tack), you become the right of way boat and can luff (in such a way that the other boat can keep clear) and thus slow the other boat down.

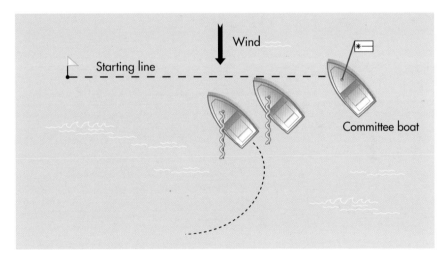

9.2b
Slotting in to leeward.

Just before the finish point, put the boat perpendicular to the line so you cross it as soon as possible. Do not do this too early and allow the boat to slow. This is your proper course, as this is how you finish in the shortest time possible. Ensure that you can clear the line afterwards.

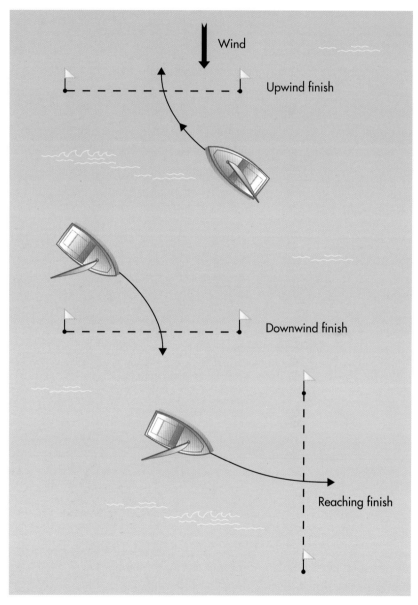

Wind

Upwind finish

Downwind finish

Reaching finish

9.2c
A quick finish.

9.3 Using the Rules Defensively

A good clean start is essential. To keep from being rolled, minimise the gap to windward to prevent the boat to windward getting a jump on you and rolling over the top. Remember the windward boat keeps clear, so do not allow boats too much room or they can roll over the top of you. If the gap is too wide, do a double tack to close the gap and create a bigger gap to leeward for yourself. Get just enough speed to tack and turn through a large angle so you do not make progress to windward.

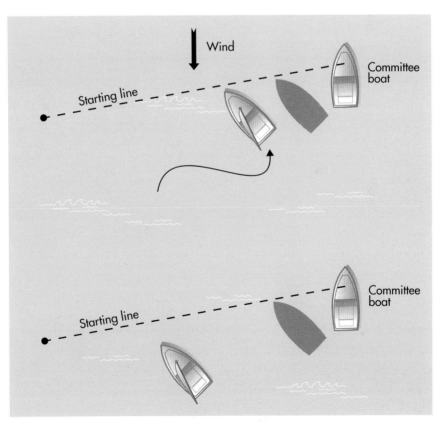

9.3a
Double tack.

To prevent a boat tacking right on your wind (the slam dunk), leave bearing away until the last minute, and then squeeze in tight just after you duck a boat (luff up towards head to wind) so the other boat has not got room to tack on you.

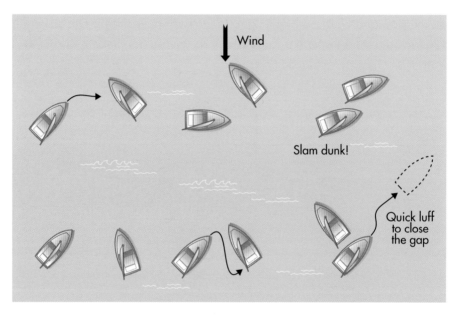

9.3b
The slam dunk.

When approaching the windward mark, sail fast and free on the lay line in the final few boat lengths so if someone tacks underneath you, you can luff and keep your wind clean, or if there is a header you can still make the mark. You do not have to alter course if boats tack in front of you until they have completed their tack. Inside the two-boat-length zone, boats cannot force you to sail above close hauled. Tacking inside the two-boat-length circle is definitely not a good idea in a tightly packed fleet.

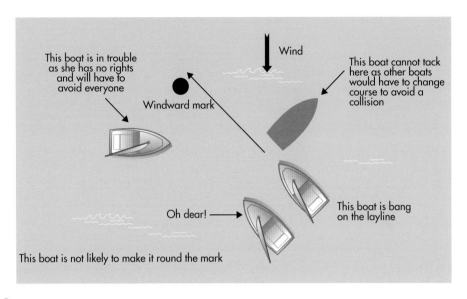

This boat is in trouble as she has no rights and will have to avoid everyone

Windward mark

Wind

This boat cannot tack here as other boats would have to change course to avoid a collision

Oh dear!

This boat is bang on the layline

This boat is not likely to make it round the mark

9.3c
Windward mark approach.

Advice from Simon Hiscocks:

The racing rules can be quite complicated and confusing. However, there aren't really that many that need to be understood. A minimum understanding, even at Olympic level, is only three rules: windward/leeward, port and starboard and rounding and passing marks. However, each of these rules includes quite a few different examples. These can be worked out pretty easily using models and the many specialist rule books.

It is all well and good understanding which boat has right of way at any given circumstance, however, in reality, there is another set of rules: what happens in real life, and how it ultimately affects the race results.

A prime example is windward/leeward in the pre-start. It is illegal for a leeward boat to come so close to a windward boat that the windward boat cannot keep clear. However, in reality, if the windward boat cannot keep clear, it either ends up in a protest or with both boats caught up in a tangle. The result of this situation is either a 50/50 protest, where it's pretty hard to prove that the right-of-way boat failed to give room, or both boats have a bad race. It is, therefore, important to understand that sometimes it is better to keep clear, even if technically you may be in the right. It is rather like using a zebra crossing: you look for traffic and check whether it is going to stop. Do you step into the road if it doesn't look as if it's going to stop? Learn the three rules and try to anticipate problems.

Meteorology

Sources of Weather Information

Understanding Weather Forecasts

Using Weather Forecasts

Advice from Joe Glanfield

10.1 Sources of Weather Information

Getting accurate weather information is a must. And there is certainly no point in obtaining inaccurate weather information! The more recent the information is, the more reliable it is likely to be. Different weather sources may be more or less reliable for different venues. Try and make looking at the forecasts part of your daily routine,

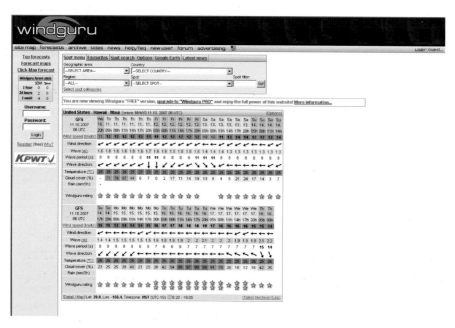

Reproduced with permission from Vaclav Hornik, WindGURU, http://www.windguru.cz/int/index.php

even when not sailing. Knowing what is going to happen, and when, is a race-winning advantage.

Practise looking at different sources of weather information and compare them with what actually happened. Some sources are better for some venues than others. Make sure you are using the right one. If possible, always get your own weather information (even if this means just watching TV and looking at the forecast on the notice board). You would be unwise just to listen to the boat park rumours!

Some regattas may have a good weather forecast displayed each day. Find out where this is posted. It is good practice to check the weather forecasts regularly as things can and do change quickly. (You probably want to be checking the notice board for race and protest times anyway.)

The weather information will come in different 'sizes' from synoptic (large systems of high and low pressures with air masses which cover thousands of square miles) to mesoscale (conditions over an area like the Solent) down to local conditions (what the wind is doing around the headland, or going to do in the next couple of hours). The latter are of most interest to the racing sailor.

If, for whatever reason, you believe the weather forecast to be highly unreliable (sometimes it can be very hard to predict the weather), the best solution may be to approach the race with a clear head and no preconceived ideas. Just observe what is happening and react to it as best you can. The weather can be frustrating, and you must not allow it to upset your mental focus.

10.2   Understanding Weather Forecasts

Once you have your weather information, it is important that you understand what it means before you can consider using it! For example, the wind forecast may just give you the gradient breeze, when in the afternoon there is a thermal effect. This could increase or decrease the wind strength and/or change the direction, depending whether it is in conflict or not.

Remember, the sun heats the earth's surface (be it land or sea), and this surface heats the air above it. Land heats quickly (although this also depends on the terrain)

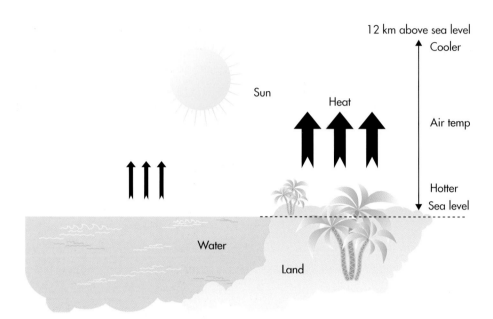

12 km above sea level

Cooler

Sun

Heat

Air temp

Hotter
Sea level

Water

Land

10.2a Heating effect.

during the day and cools quickly at night. The sea is slower to heat and cool, and therefore remains a more constant temperature throughout the day. As we move up through the atmosphere, the air cools. We sail in the bottom layer of the weather, but it is important to know what is going on above us.

It is very important to get a clear idea of what sort of day it is. This information should come from the forecast. Are things going to stay the same or change? If they are going to change, then how quickly? Will you need to keep adjusting the rig? Or do you just need to 'get your head out of the boat' and see what is going to happen? If things are going to alter, then what telltale signs are there that they are going to change? And how will you react?

Getting to a venue early can really help. On a training day try and predict what the weather is going to do. Write this down. Ask someone to get a variety of forecasts (not telling you) and write down what they think is going to happen. You can then compare notes at the end of the day.

Some forecasts give you wind arrows, which are easy to follow, but it can be more useful to look at a chart. Here, lines (like contour lines on a map) join places of equal height: these are isobars and they show equal pressure points. The high points are like hills and the lows are like valleys. The wind moves from high to low pressure, just like water running down a hill, but it follows the lines of the contours. In the northern hemisphere the wind moves slightly out from the highs and slightly in from the lows, and circulation is clockwise in a high, and anti-clockwise in a low. Remember, the closer the lines are together the steeper the gradient, and therefore the stronger the wind.

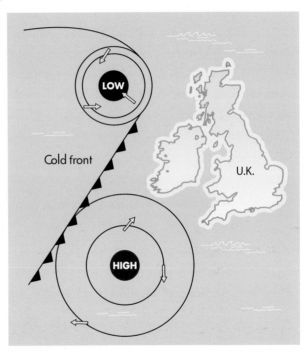

10.2b
Surface pressure forecast.

The area we sail in is called the boundary layer (the wind closest to the earth's surface); it is around 600 metres above the surface (there is no strict definition). Weather maps are for the top of the layer. They differ slightly from the bottom of the layer, where we sail, due to surface friction. However, there is a definite relationship between expected wind and the isobar spacing, so this can be very useful. (Surface wind speed will be reduced by up to 25% of the gradient and backed by up to 20 degrees over the sea. Over the land, wind speed may be reduced by as much as 75% and backed by as much as 40 degrees.)

147

However, when thinking about what is going to happen next, remember that cold fronts move approximately at the same speed as the wind (assuming all isobars are parallel) and warm fronts move at about two-thirds of this speed.

10.3 Using Weather Forecasts

Having obtained and understood the weather forecasts, we now need to use them to our best advantage. Even the best sources of information are not always accurate. If you are training alone it is better to be safe than sorry. Always make sure you can get home (training in an offshore wind can be especially dangerous). If there are large waves breaking on the shore you may need to ensure there is someone who can help you recover your boat.

The typical wind from a given direction may give you an idea of what to expect on a day:

- A north wind will be coming from the Arctic, so there is very cold, dry air moving over warmer sea, giving an unstable wind.

- A north-east wind will be polar continental. In the winter the wind will be very cold, pass over warm sea and often bring snow. In the summer warm air over cool sea brings stable air, not good for sea breezes.

- A south-east wind comes from the tropical continent (a hot landmass), which produces a stable wind.

- A south-west tropical maritime is the prevailing summer wind, which in the UK brings warm moist air over a cold sea, and sometimes foggy weather.

- The north-west polar maritime is cold air moving over a warmer sea, with unstable wind, which is often squally. Therefore a north-westerly sees a warm, wet wind, which will have lots of clouds. These you can take advantage of when racing. Big grey clouds drop down wind and rain. Sail towards this (but not behind) for more wind.

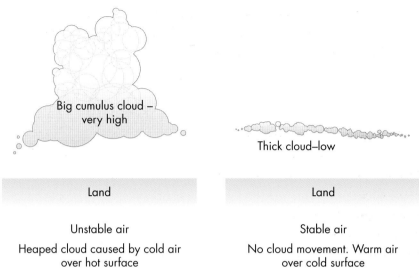

Big cumulus cloud – very high

Thick cloud–low

Land

Land

Unstable air

Stable air

Heaped cloud caused by cold air over hot surface

No cloud movement. Warm air over cold surface

10.3a
Stable and unstable air.

Stable air refers to the amount of mixing. How shifty a breeze is will also be determined by the amount of high landmass it has passed over. Big thick, cumulus clouds are a sure sign of air instability.

Big white clouds suck up wind. Avoid them at all costs; try and stay under the patches of blue sky! Head for dark clouds which are dropping wind and rain, but do not sail directly under them as you get lifted around the outside of the cloud. The clouds drop wind and rain when their height is greater than the height they are above the land/sea.

In the northern hemisphere we get several types of breezes. North-easterly breezes are wet and cold and (no surprise) they tend to come in the winter (Brrrrrrr!). In the summer we get a south-westerly wind that changes as different fronts move across. On the south coast, especially in the south west of England, the north east wind will have come over lots of land so will be especially shifty, whereas the south west wind has not passed over much land and is therefore not as shifty.

Remember, no one can get the weather forecast right all the time, and even with accurate observation the weather can be very unpredictable and may change very quickly!

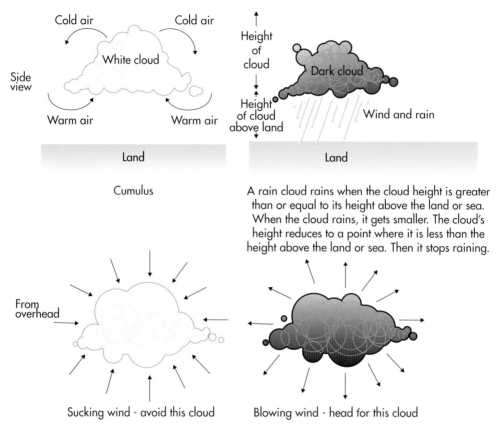

Side view

Cold air　　　Cold air

White cloud

Warm air　　　Warm air

Land

Cumulus

Height of cloud

Dark cloud

Height of cloud above land

Wind and rain

Land

A rain cloud rains when the cloud height is greater than or equal to its height above the land or sea. When the cloud rains, it gets smaller. The cloud's height reduces to a point where it is less than the height above the land or sea. Then it stops raining.

From overhead

Sucking wind - avoid this cloud

Blowing wind - head for this cloud

10.3b The effect of clouds sucking and dropping wind.

When the weather does unexpected things (and it often does), perhaps the most important thing is to be able to refocus and get on with the race (collecting as few points as possible!)

Fronts

If a front is going through, you can expect the wind to vary according to the front. Try and find out when the front is going to come through, and nearer the time look for signs of it. Clouds are formed by air lifting and cooling until the water it contains cools enough to condense. Clouds are a very useful form of information.

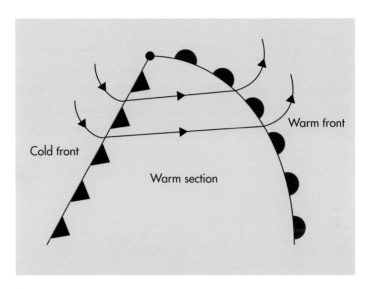

10.3c Passing fronts.

Front	Some signs (some or all may occur)
Low pressure	High cirrus clouds, the wind backs, and the barometer falls.
Approaching warm front	Cloud thickens and lowers. It then rains, and the barometer falls. The faster it falls the stronger the wind. The wind backs south and it continues to rain.
Warm front arrives	Rain breaks, and the wind veers to the south-west. The barometer steadies, and the air temperature rises, leading to steady wind from the south-west (and steady pressure), low cloud, and possible drizzle or mist.
Cold front passes	Wind backs, then increases and veers. The wind can be squally before the cloud breaks, the rain stops and the sky clears. Pressure rises suddenly.
Occluded front	Thickening and lowering of cloud; the barometer falls slowly and the rain increases as the front arrives. As the front passes you get sunshine and showers. The barometer slowly starts to rise.

Local Effects

The smaller the race course or the quicker the races, the more local any effects are. There may be just one shift a beat. In terms of your fleet positioning you may need to protect one side. If you are expecting the wind to shift that way, you should have 'a lane' and can carry on sailing without ending up being lee-bowed (a boat under you to leeward giving you bad wind) or rolled (a boat to windward giving you bad wind).

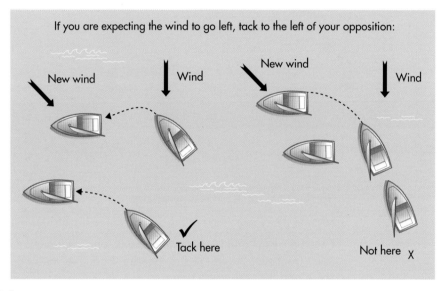

10.3d
Finding and holding a lane.

Often the last race of a series may be a medal race, which will be very short and held close to land. This means that the local topography will have more effect than the overall weather system. The wind will back over the land. If the course is close to shore this can be crucial.

If the land becomes warmer than the sea, a sea breeze can develop. There needs to be a light offshore breeze (under 15 knots) and a slack pressure gradient. If you start to see cumulus (big, white, fluffy) clouds developing over the land, there is conversion and you should expect a wind of around 15 knots, or even more, to develop.

10.3e
The land's effects on the wind for onshore and offshore winds in relation to the forecast.

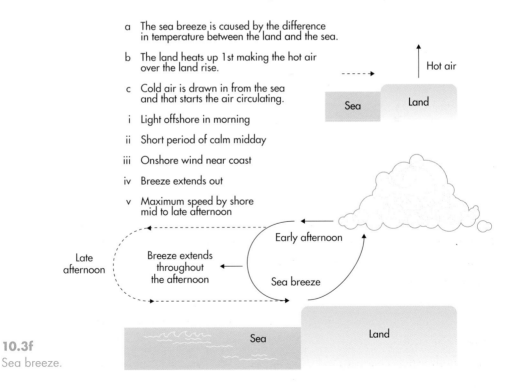

a   The sea breeze is caused by the difference in temperature between the land and the sea.

b   The land heats up 1st making the hot air over the land rise.

c   Cold air is drawn in from the sea and that starts the air circulating.

i   Light offshore in morning

ii   Short period of calm midday

iii Onshore wind near coast

iv   Breeze extends out

v   Maximum speed by shore mid to late afternoon

10.3f
Sea breeze.

Because, in general, dinghy racing is on such short courses, the Met. plays a slightly strange role in the racing we do now, but I still think it is essential to know and understand 'the golden rules' of the Met. Most dinghy racing is held very close to land, so understanding the theories of various land effects on the wind often comes into use.

I always check a weather forecast before a race day, just in case there is a change through the day. For instance, if the wind is forecast to back through the day you might push further into left shifts before tacking.

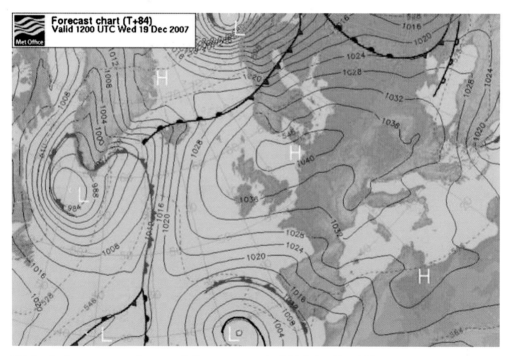

10.3g Surface pressure forecast © Crown copyright 2007, the Met Office.

Boat Speed: Upwind

Rig Set-up

Making the Boat 'Point'

Making the Boat 'Foot'

Advice from Joe Glanfield

11.1 Rig Set-up

Upwind boat speed gives you a variety of options and makes the tactics much easier. (It has been said that upwind speed makes you a tactical genius). Paying close attention to boat speed can make a real difference. It can, for example, take some of the pressure off getting a good start. The key to good boat speed is understanding your rig (sails and mast). If you are slow upwind you will find it nearly impossible to win races.

Before you even take to the water you need to ensure you have the correct kit! A mast which may be excellent for one team may be no good for another, resulting in them being over- or underpowered. The mast bend needs to match the team's righting moment (a factor of body weight and height), as well as the expected sea state and wind conditions. The more adjustable your kit is, the better. (You may choose to have a range of kit, so as to get the best set-up for different venues.)

The mast bend needs to match the luff curve of the sail. You should be able to get standard measurements from your mast manufacturer and sailmaker. At the start of a campaign always use standard kit in good condition (like the majority of the top end of the fleet). After you are comfortable with this kit, you can look for the extra edge by experimenting and tuning.

The rake of the mast is usually available through the class association. Remember, with all these rig set-ups you need to 'get your head out of the boat'. If conditions gradually change (the water becomes flatter, the wind speed increases, wave length increases, etc.) you need to adjust your rig! If you are using different sails you will need to set up the mast differently. The sailing characteristics of a full sail on a floppy mast are very different from flat sails on a stiff mast.

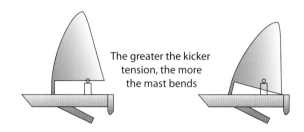

11.1a Increase the kicker tension to bend the mast.

The greater the kicker tension, the more the mast bends

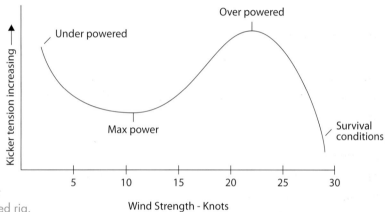

11.1b Upwind kicker tension for an unstayed rig.

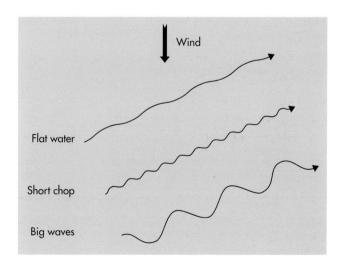

11.1c The upwind steering needs to match the waves.

Centre of effort behind centre of resistance

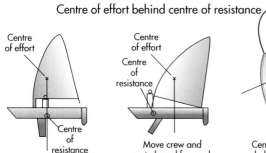

Centre of effort

Centre of resistance

Centre of effort

Centre of resistance

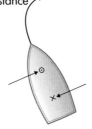

Move crew and centreboard forward. Rake rig back.

Centre of effort behind centre of resistance = boat wants to head up

- ⊙ Centre of resistance is around the crew weight and last edge of the centre board and this opposes the forces driving the boat to leeward.

- ✕ Centre of effort is around the draft (deepest/most powerful point) of the sails. This has some force to leeward as well as driving the boat forward.

- ⚬ Crew
  ⌂

Centre of effort in front of centre of resistance

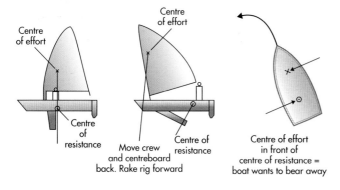

Centre of effort

Centre of effort

Centre of resistance

Centre of resistance

Move crew and centreboard back. Rake rig forward

Centre of effort in front of centre of resistance = boat wants to bear away

Centre of effort over centre of resistance

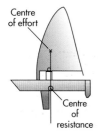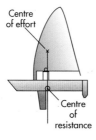

Centre of effort

Centre of effort

Centre of resistance

Centre of resistance

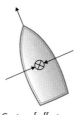

Centre of effort over centre of resistance = boat wants to go in a straight line

11.1d Centre of effort in relation to the centre of resistance.

In an unstayed rig (a Laser, for example, which does not have shrouds) the mast is bent by the kicker see figure 11.1a. The boom is pressed into the lower mast (this does not happen with a vang lever) and the top of the sail is pulled backwards. In medium airs the leach tension is governed by the sheet tension. In light and strong winds the rig needs to be depowered. In light winds because the wind needs an 'easier' sail to get around, and in strong winds because the sailor needs to be able to keep the boat flat. This is achieved by adjusting the kicker.

If the conditions are constantly changing, you need to be constantly changing the rig so that it is optimised for the conditions. If the conditions are constant, set your rig as best you can and then leave it, so you can concentrate on other things. When conditions are constantly changing you need a set-up which is easy to sail (in other words, it is easy to point, foot and make the boat go fast in a range of wind speeds).

First let's get the fundamentals right. You really need to do a comprehensive test of the available kit in a range of conditions to find out what is best for you. However, the table below gives the key ideas:

Sail fundamentals.

Flat water	Flat sails	Less power required
Choppy water	Fuller sail	More power required
Flat water	Tight leach	
Choppy water	Leach twist	

Steering

Once the rig is set up we need to look at steering see figure 11.1c. The steering needs to match the waves. The frequency of steering correlates with the wave length: the closer together the waves, the more frequently you need to steer (until the point when the waves are so close together that you can no longer steer accurately). The angle of steering is:

Examples:

- Flat water: small (smooth) but frequent movements, to keep the boat at the optimum angle to the wind. Allow windward telltale to just lift. (Would suit a flat sail with a hard leach.)

- Short chop: small, rapid (choppy) steering movements, to keep the bow from slamming. (Would suit sailing the boat low and fast to minimise speed lost from hitting the occasional wave.)

- Big waves: slow, steady (smooth) steering with large angle changes, to keep the boat in contact with the waves. (Would suit a full sail with leach twist.)

The principles of steering are always the same upwind: minimising the time spent going uphill (luffing up the waves) and maximising the time going downhill (bearing away down the waves). This also builds speed to go back up the waves. A good rig set-up will make it easy to sail through the desired angles. You can also use your body movement to help trim the boat over the waves, pulling your weight back to lift the bow and moving forwards to keep the bow in the water. You want as smooth a transit as possible to get over the waves. (If you are slamming down

on the waves, you may well lose height as the wind gets under the bow – move your weight forwards. Conversely if you are burying the bow and most likely going slow – move your weight back).

Moving the crew weight back and raking the centreboard moves the centre of resistance back. Moving the crew weight forward and raking the centreboard forward moves the centre of resistance forward. Moving the fullness in the sail forward makes the boat want to bear away; moving it back makes the boat want to head up. It may be useful to have the extreme of these set-ups if you really want to go low or high, but generally the best set-up is

to have the centre of effort directly over the centre of resistance.

Get to know your rig so you can get it to both point and foot.

11.2   Making the Boat 'Point'

Being able to sail close to the wind without losing speed to windward is called pointing. This is when the boat is feathered or pinched through the wind, sailing the closest angle to the wind possible without losing significant boat speed. This is especially relevant when coming off the start line and having to hold your lane. By sailing the boat 'high' you are unlikely to fall into the boat to leeward and end up in a lee-bow position.

Here the rig set-up is to have a full sail with enough power to get through the waves or the chop. A tight leach to 'sail off', the boat trim well forward and the boat balance flat or even slightly to windward all help keep the foils working efficiently.

There is a limit where you create too much power and the associated drag makes the boat slip sideways. We are interested in the track the boat is making over the water, not where the bow is actually pointing. When a boat is sailing fast for the conditions the foils work more efficiently, thus the boat will make less ground to leeward.

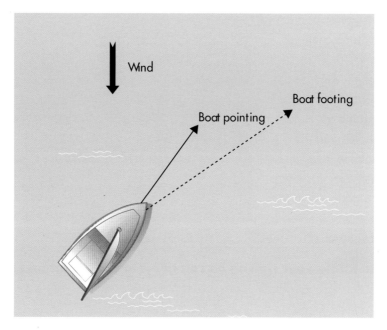

11.2a Boat pointing too high and slipping sideways compared with a boat sailing well.

Therefore, in order to gain height, you must bear away a little bit every so often to keep the speed on. Making the boat point assumes you are still making good VMG (velocity made good). It will rarely pay to point really high and have poor VMG, unless you are likely to lose lots of ground by putting in two tacks.

A tight leach provides power and pointing ability.

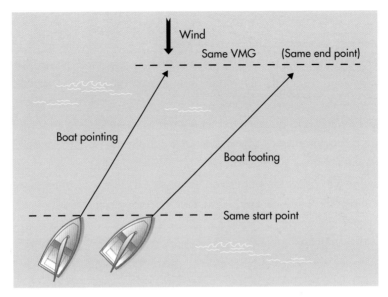

11.2b Boats with different and the same VMG.

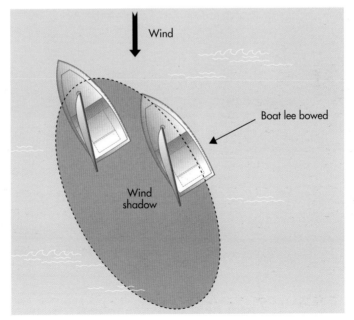

11.2c Lee bow.

11.3 Making the Boat 'Foot'

Sometimes it is necessary to really drive the boat to get over to some pressure, a shift, out of the current or over the top of another boat. Here you need to turn distance to windward into speed, sacrificing height for speed and sailing so low that you are almost reaching.

The boat trim needs to be back to allow the bow to lift slightly, making it easier to keep the boat born away (bow down). The sails need to be flat so that gusts will not tend to make you luff, and it may even be worth raking the foils back as well.

You may have to allow the boat to come up slightly every so often to lose power. This is better than constantly pulling on the tiller, as it means the rudder is acting as a slight brake (when the rudder is straight it provides the minimum resistance).

It may well pay to foot on one tack and pinch on the other (perhaps to get across to one side of the race course, or maybe so as to get a good angle of attack to the waves). If this is the case, you need to be ready to make the changes to your rig promptly.

Leach twist provides speed.

Advice from Joe Glanfield:

A lot of upwind boat speed in technical boats comes from good consistent settings. Normally nothing special, but a question of having your boat well calibrated so you are able to put the controls in the right place for the right condition, and then repeat it the next day. To transfer this onto a race course, good communication (on a double-handed boat) is key, especially when the wind is inconsistent. It needs to be one sailor's responsibility to call in the gusts and lulls so the other sailor can adjust the controls to match. Often sailors struggle to transfer tuning speed to the race course. This is normally because both sailors are looking around too much whilst racing, when actually just one sailor could do the majority of looking around whilst the other concentrates on the boat speed.

In our boat I concentrate on the tactics so Nick never has to look outside the boat and can just focus on steering and sail settings. I believe that the communication between me and Nick and our clearly defined roles in the boat are the main reasons we are fast across the wind range.

Boat Speed: Reaching

Rig Set-up

'Soaking' Low

Going for Speed

Advice from Simon Hiscocks

12.1 Rig Set-up

The setting changes from upwind to reaching need to be done as efficiently as possible at the windward mark, or, if possible, very slightly beforehand. The fundamental rig set-up does not change from that of the upwind (for example, you are looking for flatter sails on a windier day).

Rig set-up for going low may mean creating as much power in the rig as possible (full sails), whereas going for speed may mean flatter sails. Mast rake will, in most cases, already be set and is optimised for the upwind legs of the course.

The leach tension will determine how easy it is to head up/bear away. Consider that in most conditions you sail with more kicker upwind than downwind. On a reach this certainly holds true. To help the boat head up, add kicker. This pulls the centre of effort back in the sail, making the boat want to point up. If you let the kicker off it is easier to bear away.

In breezy conditions, having the kicker off prior to gybing can help prevent the boom from hitting the water, effectively sheeting in the sail and capsizing the boat as it 'trips' over the boom. Ideally, before getting to a mark, you will have decided whether you are going high or low (for whatever reason) and get the rig set up accordingly.

Boat trim is adjusted according to wind strength and wave height. The higher the waves, the more you move the crew weight back for any given wind strength. When the wind is light, the trim needs to be well forward to allow the smooth flow of water from the transom. However, be careful not to over trim the bow, resulting in the hull having to 'push more water out of the way'. In medium conditions you are looking for maximum waterline length up to the point when the boat can plane. Weight then shifts as far aft as possible without dragging the transom.

12.2 'Soaking' Low

Soaking is getting the boat to point as low as possible without losing speed. For tactical or strategic reasons you may want to soak low, perhaps to prevent a boat

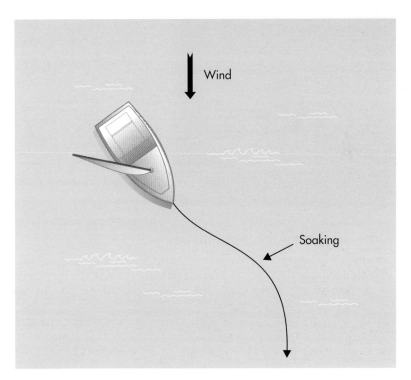

12.2a Soaking.

from getting inside you at the next mark (tactical consideration) or to get out of an adverse tidal flow (strategic consideration). You may want to soak below the lay line if you think the wind or tide is going to change across the leg.

Think about how the boat 'feels'. You need to try and bear away to the point where the speed seems to be affected As soon as there is the slightest slowing, you need to come back up again. It is far more efficient to keep an average speed rather than constantly having to accelerate the boat.

When going low you need to have clear breeze. There is no point going slightly low only to be rolled over by other boats which take your wind. You want to be several boat lengths (in an ideal world, six mast heights) to leeward of boats to windward.

To bear away initially, you need to use a small amount of windward heel to help the boat come off the wind without using too much rudder. However, the boat needs to be flat when going in its new target direction. If you need to get back up slightly (you are running out of pressure, for example), move the crew weight inboard to create slight leeward heel and allow the boat to come up to its new target direction. Now return the crew weight to the 'neutral' position so the boat continues in a straight line. Remember, all boats sail fast with minimum 'corrective' steerage. (Having to use the rudder to correct the course is the result of poor trimming.)

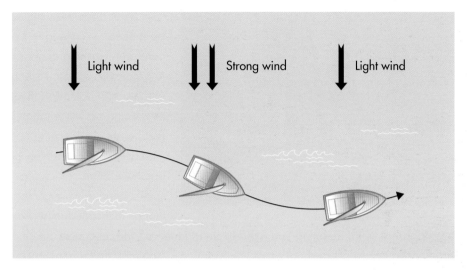

12.2b Going high in the lulls and low in the gusts.

Keeping your average speed high is very important, as it is far more efficient than accelerating in the gusts and allowing the boat to slow down in the lulls. Ideally, keep the trimming, steering and body movements in time with changes in the wind. Make frequent small changes, and where possible try to anticipate what is going to happen next.

12.3   Going for Speed

For tactical or strategic reasons you may want to go fast and high, perhaps to prevent a boat from rolling over the top of you and taking your breeze (tactical consideration) or to get up to a band of stronger wind (strategic consideration).

Boats go faster when they are 'on their own'. This is partly because of the way the breeze behaves (it would prefer to go over one sail rather than several), but mainly because it is easier for the boat to sail the best course (bearing away in the gusts, heading up in the lulls) when not battling with other boats for position.

Think about how the boat 'feels': you need to be constantly pushing the boat up to gain extra speed. As soon as you are not increasing the pace by coming up further, then keep that height. As the wind speed increases and decreases the optimum angle can change significantly. Also remember that as hull speed increases, so does apparent wind, meaning you need to sheet in more (and, of course, sheet out when the speed comes off and apparent wind reduces). You may find when the boat is at full pace you can bear away slightly without losing speed. Do this to maximise VMG (velocity made good, or simply the speed for getting close to the next mark).

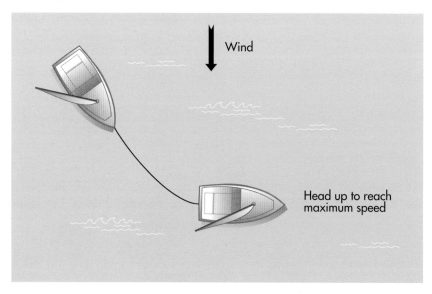

12.3a Going for speed.

You need to be careful when you go high to make sure that you can still gybe in front of the boats behind (depending upon how long it takes you to complete a gybe and your rights afterwards). You may need to soak slightly for a couple of boat lengths before going for the gybe to ensure you do not infringe boats behind. (Remembering, of course, that you always want to have good pace to complete a gybe!)

Good speed often comes from when you are truly in tune with the boat and subconsciously driving it. When you get stressed and try too hard to get the boat going, you often end up making the boat go slower (unless perhaps it is very windy, thus rewarding aggressive sailing).

The best way to improve reaching speed is to do very long tuning runs. Try and sail for 20 minutes (much longer than you would do in a normal race) on one reach

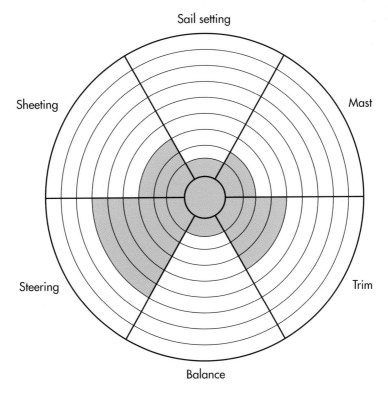

12.3b Reaching dartboards.

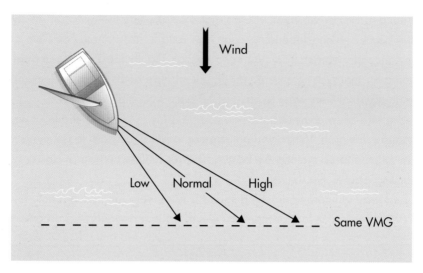

12.3c VMG explained (three courses with same VMG).

with a consistent average heading. Make sure you do the reach on both tacks. Try and discover what condition you find the most difficult. Is it tight reaching in strong winds? Beam reaching with the waves side on? Broad reaching in light winds? Then, whenever possible, practise in these conditions!

Advice from Simon Hiscocks:

Due to the normal course configurations, asymmetric skiffs rarely reach. It could be argued that skiffs always reach downwind, which is a reasonable assumption. Let us consider what is happening between a boat trying to sail low and one that is trying to sail high to lay a mark (i.e. a proper reach and an apparent wind downwind run).

Wind is wind, so whether it is true wind or apparent wind it still has the same effect of an air mass hitting a boat's rig at a given wind speed. Therefore, if a boat goes faster it gets more wind. Lightweight skiffs tend to sail fastest on a run by sailing as fast as possible. This creates more wind (air mass hitting the boat) and the effect is better velocity made good (actual speed towards the next mark).

Conversely, if the boat is sailing higher than is required, slowing it down will reduce the amount of wind that hits the boat's rig. Less wind will mean less power, so the boat can sail closer to the wind. The closer to the wind the boat sails, the slower it will go. This means that it's possible to slow down by sailing closer to the wind. Of course, there is a limit to this. Taken to an extreme, the boat either capsizes or ends up head to wind. Hence, there is a fine line when trying to sail too high with the kite up.

Keeping all the sails well eased will help reduce power. And, depending on how secure the mast is, pulling on the cunningham will also help. (The 49er mast is not secure enough for this!) Over easing the kite has the effect of folding the luff back on itself, which helps to reduce power, but it does need a fair bit of sheeting in and out to control. Lastly, keep as much weight out as possible to create maximum leverage, and slow down by heading up to create leeward heel.

Be careful of the rudder stalling. If and when it does stall, flow can be reattached by straightening the rudder angle to the centre line. This might feel a bit odd as it will probably feel like heading up. Dumping the kite will also help. Good communication between helm and crew is essential.

Boat Speed: Running

Rig Set-up

Sailing by the Lee

Apparent Wind Sailing

Advice from Paul Goodison

Gone are the days when the downwind leg was a chance for a quick rest! Often races are finished downwind, or after a very small beat/reach to the finish, so downwind speed is more important than ever (especially now most regatta formats are more but shorter races). Downwind legs can be just as physical, if not more physical, than the upwind legs. When training you should train aerobically for the whole length of the race (60 minutes if you are a Laser sailor), not just 20 minutes (the typical length of the first beat).

13.1 Rig Set-up

The rig needs to be set up to provide a stable platform so the boat is always driving forward (perhaps with a small amount of lift at the bow), rather than being pushed either to windward or leeward. You do not want to waste the energy of the wind tipping the boat on its side rather than driving the boat forward. The foils should be raised to reduce friction but still provide a turning point for the boat.

A good rig set-up gives you lots of feel. Remember, to have the same leach twist in 15 knots, you will require more kicker tension than in 5 knots. The pressure in the sail is increased by the square of the wind speed, and the more pressure in the sail the more the leach wants to open. Remember to 'get your head out of the boat' to look at the wind, so you can try and make the adjustments before the wind changes. The sail control which gets the most adjustment is probably the kicker.

The waves will rarely be lined up with the wind, so one tack may be better than another for surfing the waves. You need to get a rig set-up which allows the boat to head up and bear away through the appropriate angle. (Basically the more kicker, the easier it is to get the boat to head up, but the harder it is to get it to bear away, and vice versa).

Telltales can help to tell you whether your sail is correctly trimmed: they should stream from the luff towards the leach, ideally horizontally. If they are drooping on the windward side you need to sheet in. If the telltales on the leeward side are drooping you need to sheet out. They should be placed approximately six mast diameters from

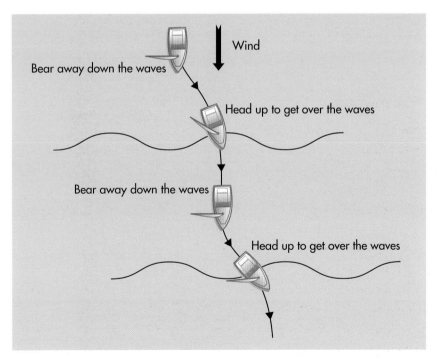

13.1a Heading up and bearing away for the waves.

the luff of the sail at a variety of heights. Leach telltales can also be useful for fully battened sails on stayed rigs.

When sailing upwind you are looking for the lifting tack, that is the tack which is taking you closest to the windward mark. On the run you are, therefore, looking for the heading tack (you gybe to stay 'in phase' with the wind) to take you as close as possible to the leeward mark.

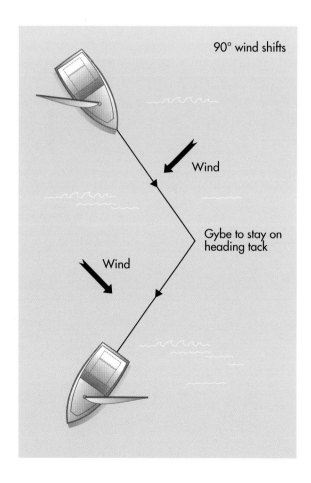

90° wind shifts

Wind

Gybe to stay on heading tack

Wind

13.1b Choosing the heading tack downwind.

13.2 Sailing by the Lee

Unstayed rigs like that of the Laser reward sailing by the lee. Here the flow of wind is going from the leach to the mast (rather than the other way around). The mast is now acting like the leach, and because it is stiffer than the sail it is more stable.

When you are running by the lee, telltales will go the opposite way (they should stream from the leach pointing towards the luff). They also respond the opposite way, so if the windward telltale is drooping you need to sheet out.

By sailing by the lee followed by broad reaching, boats can sail a large range of angles, which can be useful for catching/avoiding waves. It also means you have a greater freedom of movement as you do not need to keep on gybing. Try and use as thin a mainsheet as you can, so you can really feel the pressure in the sail (and know when it is switching).

You may find it fastest to sail by the lee, so you may end up gybing on the shifts, just as you would when sailing downwind on a broad reach. Absolute dead running is

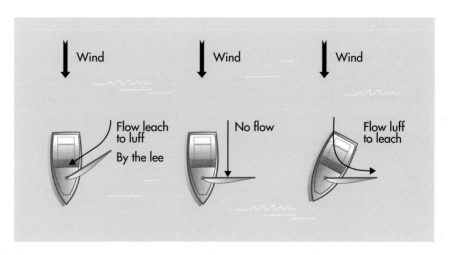

13.2a Flow of wind over the sail (leach to luff, straight on and luff to leach).

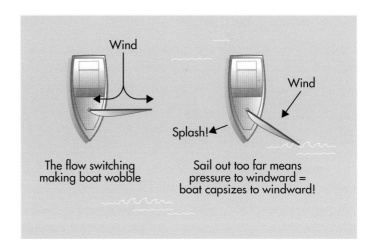

Wind

Wind

Splash!

The flow switching
making boat wobble

Sail out too far means
pressure to windward =
boat capsizes to windward!

13.2b Death roll.

rarely fast, as flow over the sail (whether from luff to leach or leach to luff) is faster and more stable.

The death roll is often caused by the boat being more or less straight downwind and the wind switching direction over the sail, or when the boat is straight downwind and the sail is let out too far, so the pressure is now exerted to windward.

A boat may well switch between sailing for a few waves broad reaching, running through a gap, and then sailing by the lee to avoid the next couple of waves. This can avoid the potential loss when gybing.

If you were trying to follow the boat closely from behind in a RIB, you would see it zigzagging all over the place. However, if you were a long way above the boat (in a helicopter!) it would appear to be sailing a straight line more or less directly downwind.

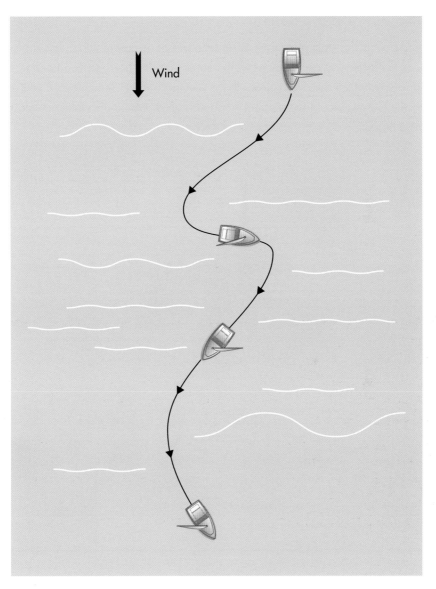

13.2c Boat sailing downwind using the waves.

13.3 Apparent Wind Sailing

High-speed downwind sailing involves large amounts of apparent wind. This is arguably a reach, as the faster you go the more wind comes from the front, so you need to sheet in or bear away (which takes you closer to the leeward mark). Remember, if you are sailing by the lee you would sheet out or head up (which would also take you closer to the leeward mark).

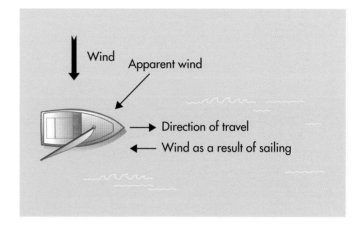

13.3a Apparent wind.

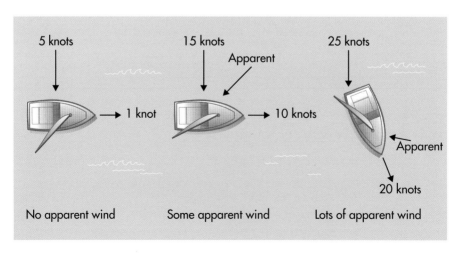

13.3b Increasing apparent wind.

However, to get the boat to go fast you need to head up more, or bear away more and sail by the lee (harder in boats with unstayed rigs). By doing so, you go faster but have to sail a greater distance. Remember, as the boat slows down you lose your apparent wind.

Generally speaking, slower boats will always sail by the true wind, whilst fast boats with asymmetric spinnakers will always sail by apparent wind. However, many boats fall in between, sailing mainly off true wind in light winds with apparent wind becoming more of a factor in the upper wind range. The higher the performance the sooner apparent wind sailing occurs.

The most important thing for downwind boat speed is pressure: the more wind we have and the longer we can stay in it, the faster the boat will go. To spend the most time in the pressure it is important to sail in the direction that the pressure is travelling, and then link up the next area of pressure without spending too much time in the lighter spot. Waves are also critical to increase boat speed. Try and keep the boat travelling down the front of waves as much as possible, and spend as little time as possible travelling up the back of them. In Laser sailing it is important to use the heel of the boat to assist steering, as using too much rudder will slow the boat down. Make sure the boat is heeled to windward on the bear away and heeled to leeward on the luff ups.

Fitness

What is Fitness?

How Fit Do You Need to Be?

How to Improve Your Fitness

Advice from Paul Goodison

14.1 What is Fitness?

Fitness is the ability to do the job you set out to do. This is obviously very different (but perhaps no more or less demanding), depending on whether you are a Laser sailor, a keelboat grinder or a 49er crew. At the top level you want to be as fit as you can be, and peak for your key regattas in the year (for example, World or European Championships), allowing some down time afterwards (whether you feel you need it or not) to recover. As a guide, you should aim to peak no more than three times a year (it can take up to 16 weeks to get to peak fitness) and have at least three down times a year (of around 5–7 days).

So what are the aspects of fitness? Well, there are many words used to describe things, and some go in and out of fashion, but an easy way to remember the elements of fitness are the four 'Ss'. Analyse your role within the boat and decide which of them are important for you!

Strength: both the ability to lift a very heavy load once, and a light load lots of times.

Speed: the ability to be quick across the boat.

Suppleness: the ability to flex, and general mobility around the boat.

Stamina: the ability to keep going and recover well (cardiovascular fitness).

You can see that one without the other is no good at all. Being fast but not very supple means your boat handling will be fast but not smooth. As a bare minimum you need to be strong enough to 'do the job'. Whatever your role, it is inadvisable to score extremely low in any of the Ss, as it may make normal life activities more difficult.

Let us have a look at a couple of examples, using our dartboards for the four 'Ss':

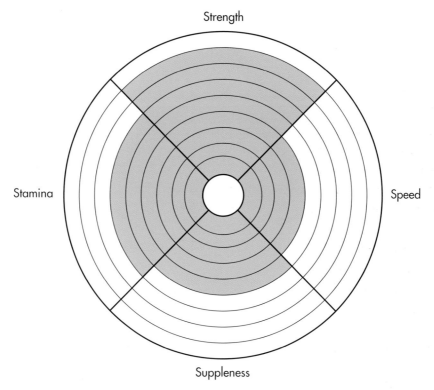

14.1a Dartboard for a keelboat crew.

You need to have the correct fitness for your role within the boat. If you do not, you must consider which is easier to change – your fitness or your role? A young

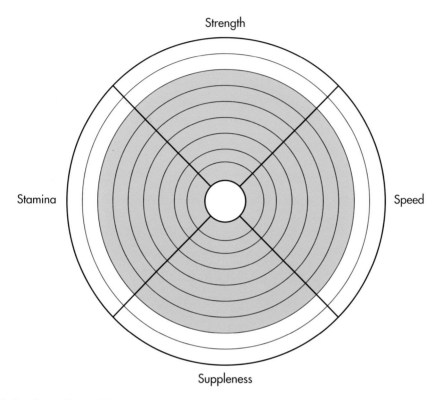

14.1b Dartboard for a 49er crew.

sailor may grow up being helm, but once adult be better suited to crewing, for example. Look at members of your family to help forecast the size and build you are likely to become.

If you are changing your role it is often advisable to work on the fitness requirement before you actually change classes. This way, when you start in the new boat your performance will not be limited by lack of fitness. If you try out a new sport for fun (such as skiing) you may well ache afterwards if you do not do a bit of training beforehand. Limit this by being well prepared, or make sure you do not go skiing (or whatever) just before an important event.

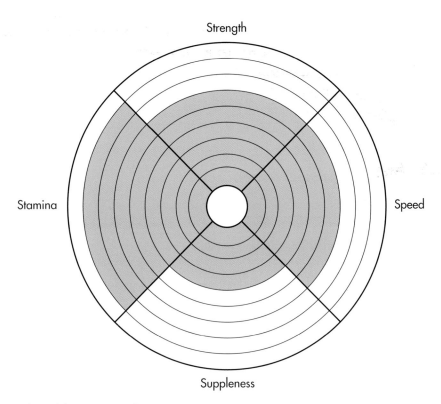

Strength

Stamina

Speed

Suppleness

14.1c Dartboard for a Laser sailor.

14.2 How Fit Do You Need to Be?

In an ideal world you would gain all your fitness from sailing. However, this is not usually possible as the wind is not as reliable as a running track! It is also very expensive in both time and money to get out on the water. In comparison, gym membership fees and a pair of good trainers (replace after every 500 miles run) may seem like pocket money!

You need to be fit enough to do your job: this means you must be suited to the boat you sail. Extreme dieting or weight gain are not healthy. Changes in body weight (through training and diet) need to be achieved gradually over a period of time. When you are away at regattas your body will try and return to its natural weight, so if you are well above or below this, you will find it increasingly hard when doing lots of sailing (see Chapters 15 and 16 for more detail).

If you are not fit enough, it will affect your concentration (see Chapter 19), as your focus will be on the pain in your legs rather than the wind shift to the right! The winter, when it is harder to be getting time in on the water, is often a good time to improve your fitness.

14.3   How to Improve Your Fitness

A good training session has a beginning, a middle and an end. If you are pushed for time, do not be tempted just to do the middle bit! If time is too short, train the following day or complete just half of the middle routine.

Each training session must have a specific goal. If you try and do everything on one day you will limit your possible improvements. Good nutrition and rest are vital, and sometimes having more time between workouts will improve your gains. Overtraining is a sure way to illness and injury.

The squat–a muscle building exercise for the entire lower body.

The beginning of a session is the warm up. This is exactly what it says it is! You gradually warm up the body to the point of a slight sweat. This prepares the body for exercise. Your muscles are like a piece of toffee. When warm it stretches easily, but try bending the same piece of toffee when it has just come out of the fridge. It snaps. I think I've made my point!

Injury prevention is a key part of good training. It can seem to take forever to get fit,

Polar S610 heart rate monitor. (Used with permission from Polar Electro UK Ltd.)

but it takes just one silly mistake to lose fitness due to injury. Always wear appropriate clothing, and use good technique. If you do not have time to do a session properly don't do it. Skipping the warm up in the beginning or the stretching at the end is not an option. You can, however, do less. (If you were going to do chest and back, then perhaps you could just do chest now and do back at the next opportunity you get.)

Light stretching (for around 10 seconds) is advisable as part of the warm up, but it is the warm up itself which is the most important part. At the end of the session we have a cool down. Here you can do the developmental stretches (lasting 30 seconds or more) to help improve your suppleness. You can also get the help of a training partner to push the stretch even further. Stretch for 10 seconds, relax and then get your partner to push the stretch slightly. Repeat three times (or more).

So what is the meat in the sandwich? Well, this is the part where you make specific performance improvements.

Training for Laser Hiker

Laser sailors need to be able to hike for long periods of time. The best way is to spend lots of time on the water. Failing that, exercises which use a large amount of leg strength, such as cycling, are ideal. The time spent on the bike needs to equal or exceed the expected length of the race (about an hour), and equal or exceed the intensity (measured with a heart-rate monitor).

Training the muscles around the knee is very important as they allow for straight leg hiking. Knee pain is likely to occur if you hike with bent legs. Another issue, which is more common now, is the ankle pain associated with hiking with a pointed toe. The toe should be at a neutral angle (neither pointing straight up nor straight down) for a balanced approach.

Hiking bench–so you can do a sailing-specific training indoors (for a few minutes each day) when you cannot get out on the water.

Training for 49er Crew

Explosiveness is required for crews who have to do hoists and drops. The loads trained with need to be higher than those experienced whilst racing. Grip strength is also important, as if the grip fails there is a lot of wasted effort. (Make sure you use good grippy gloves, which you can buy cheaply from any hardware store.)

Aerobic activity should involve pulls. Rowing is a great example: it uses a large number of muscle groups (making it easier to achieve a high heart rate) without being high impact (like running).

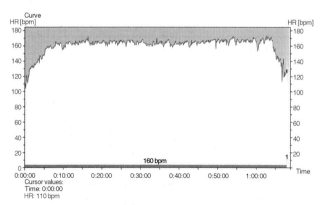

Polar heart rate graph (to check if you are training at the right intensity). (Used with permission from Polar Electro UK Ltd.)

It is very important to look after the lower back. This requires a strong set of abdominals, so that you can pull in a variety of angles while keeping the back stable. If you experience back pain coming off the water, a good stretch will help keep the lumbar curve in your back. Lie face forward on the ground and, keeping your pelvis on the floor, raise your chest using your arms – like doing a press-up).

Training for Keelboats

If you are winching or pulling on ropes, try and train specifically. For example, do chin ups using a rope, or pull a rope at the same angle as you would on the boat, using the same hand position. However, it is still advisable to do some sort of general circuit training as well.

For all Sailors

In addition to specific training you may well need to do supportive training to avoid any muscle imbalances if your main physical activity is sailing. Think about good posture on and off the water. Address any aches and pains sooner rather than later, as they could be a result of poor technique and/or overtraining.

To move your training on, you need always to be pushing to reach the next level. Remember TTIF when considering types of gradual increase to improve performance:

Time: increase the duration of the activity. Perform extra time on the rower, extra sets or reps in the gym and extra hours on the water.

Type: change the type of exercise you are doing. This may just be for interest's sake! Even a small difference can help. Go for doing squats with the bar behind the neck (back squat) to holding the bar in front of the chest (front squat), or change your normal cycle for a reclined bike.

Intensity: increase the intensity. This may be a small amount every week or large jumps each month. As the intensity grows, the time may need to decrease. To increase intensity, increase the heart rate or the weight, or decrease the rest between sets.

Frequency: increase the number of training sessions per week as fitness improves and less recovery is required.

Young sailors need to be cautious when starting a weight training routine. Heavy weights (those over 70% of the maximum weight you can lift once, known as the one repmax) are the maximum which should be attempted. (If you may still be growing and you cannot lift a weight three times, you should not be lifting it.)

However, starting young can build good technique, which can be very helpful for later life. For example, using a broom handle instead of a bar (which weighs 20 kilograms) you can learn good technique for Power lifting (chest press, squat, deadlift) and Olympic lifting (clean and jerk, snatch). Free weight training should always involve a spotter, even with light weights.

Working the core is also very important; you are never too young to start building a solid middle and improving aerobic fitness. In times of injury, it is important to keep on working on these areas if at all possible. The abdomen is what connects the upper to the lower body, so this needs to be solid. It is important therefore, to use a fit ball to work on the inner muscles. When squatting, for example, it is advisable not to wear a belt for the lighter movements. This will help with training the stomach muscles. However, you should use a belt for heavy lifts in order to protect the lower back.

Training the opposite muscles is important. If one group of muscles is very tight they can pull the joints into bad posture (for example, pulling the shoulder position backwards if you overtrain the back or forwards if you overtrain the chest. Be aware that you are only as strong as your weakest link, which may be grip. Whether you are training in the gym or racing, make sure you get the required support from your clothing.

Advice from Paul Goodison:

Fitness is becoming an ever more important part of sailing, often making the difference between winning and losing. It is important to realise what sort of fitness is needed for a specific role in the boat. If the training is not specific to your sailing, it will be less effective. You need to set a realistic plan of how much training you can actually fit into your normal life, and when the plan is set, stick to it.

The key to a successful routine is continuity: it is much better to do a little more often than do lots sporadically. When training in the gym get a training partner to spot for you and give encouragement. This helps to get the most out of each session. Exercise is easier if it is stimulating and fun. I try to vary my aerobic training as much as possible: cycling in a group helps the hours fly by, cross-training, such as playing tennis and squash, helps to improve a basic level of aerobic fitness. If training is fun it is going to be easier to complete than when you don't feel motivated.

Diet

Understanding Nutritional Labelling

What We Need to Eat

Diet Suggestions

Advice from Joe Glanfield

Just like everyone else, sailors need a good balanced diet. Not only will you sail faster if you are fit and healthy, but life is simply easier. (No more getting out of breath running up a few steps to catch your flight!) Your diet will not only affect you physically but also your mental focus. Even if you stop sailing, a good diet is well worth having.

In this chapter diet means our day-to-day eating (at home, on holiday and at championships), not reducing calorie intake in order to lose weight (see Chapter 16).

Even out of the competition season it makes sense to follow a healthy diet. Eating lots of fruit and vegetables forms a good habit; just ensure you wash them carefully. If you are rushed for time, do not take the easy option and grab a takeaway, or put off eating until later. (Your body will operate best on small meals often, rather than larger, infrequent meals). Prepare some healthy sandwiches, pasta salads, or risotto, plus fruit, which you can eat throughout the day.

There is a psychological aspect to eating, and a specific diet should never be seen as a reward or a punishment. Likewise, being fit, being healthy and being fat are separate issues. Fitness (see Chapter 14) is mainly governed by physical activity. Health is governed by diet, and fatness is governed by calories (see Chapter 16). You could, for example, be your target weight but not have a good diet. (You could save all your calories and use them in the evening for puddings and alcohol.) Or you could have a large amount of body fat but still be physically very fit (perhaps when you are having to gain weight rapidly).

Although it is hard to measure, a good diet will help your performance. It is not only what you see on the outside of the body (muscle structure, flat stomach) that is important but also how well your organs are functioning on the inside. The liver, for example, is one of the body's 'power sources' – and that makes a difference. So, make sure you give it the correct fuel!

15.1   Understanding Nutritional Labelling

In recent years, the quality of information on food packaging has improved by leaps and bounds. Several supermarkets have gone to increasingly high levels to make it obvious what is good (or not good) for you to eat in large quantities. In order to understand your diet you just need to understand the basics. Deep down most people inherently know what is good or bad for them; they may just choose to ignore it.

However, be aware that food labels may be misleading. A low sugar food may have lots of fat in it, or a low fat food may have lots of sugar in it! Products with 50% less fat may still contain a lot of fat. Do not assume that you can eat huge amounts of foods which claim to be from a supermarket's 'healthy' range. There is room in a healthy diet for all food types, but some need to be restricted to a little every so often.

Carbohydrates

These should form the majority of your diet, around 60% or 70% at a regatta. They are best taken from whole food sources rather than refined foods. Two hours prior to racing, a complex (starch) carbohydrate food – made mainly from wholemeal rice, bread, pasta or cereal – is an ideal meal. Immediately prior to the race

and straight after (perhaps 30 minutes), a simple (sugar) carbohydrate snack, such as bananas, would be good.

So perhaps a regatta day looks like this:

8:30	Porridge for breakfast
10:30	A couple of bananas
11:00	Race 1 followed by a carbohydrate drink (5–8 grams of carbohydrate per 100 ml fluid)
12:00	Race 2 followed by a carbohydrate drink (5–8 grams of carbohydrate per 100 ml fluid)
13:00	Race 3 followed by a carbohydrate drink
15:00	Return ashore for light pasta/sandwich
18:00	Dinner containing meat and lots of vegetables
20:00	Dinner 2 on a windy regatta

Protein

Protein is essential for recovery. The body uses it to repair itself when resting. A low protein diet will usually lead to the loss of lean tissue (muscle). Good sources of protein are lean red meat, fish, poultry and eggs. Protein should make up around 20% of your diet. Try and eat protein little and often (egg for breakfast, tuna sandwich for lunch, and turkey breast for dinner), rather than eating a huge steak at the end of the day. Protein takes longer to digest than carbohydrate and uses more water.

Getting good quality proteins can be harder for vegetarians as you need a complete set of amino acids, which you do not get just from beans, for example. Soya milk has one amino acid missing, which you find in dairy products. But often the people who have soya take it because they are lactose-intolerant! So you need to mix nuts, beans, pulses and cereals. A good meal would be something like beans on toast, as the combination of pulses and cereals gives a complete amino acid mix.

Fats

Fats are not bad! They are essential for your body to function properly. However, fats that are liquid at room temperature (oils) are better than those which are completely solid (saturated fats). Olive, rape and sunflower oils are definitely part of a healthy diet and should make up around 20%. Solid fats, like lard, should be avoided. Never consume hydrogenated fats (those which were liquid oils but have had hydrogen added to make them solid). However, during a regatta the demand for carbohydrate (for fuel) and protein (for repair) is increased, so fat probably drops to around 10% of your diet. Gram for gram, fat contributes twice as many calories as protein or carbohydrates.

Salt

A special mention should be made of salt. It is an important part of any diet but may be found in high levels in processed food, which is another reason for avoiding it. Salt is added to enhance taste, especially of foods with little taste (for example, corn flakes). So an otherwise healthy food can contain far too much salt. When the sugar or fat content of a product has been reduced, salt may be added to make the product more tasty! The closer food is to its starting form the better. (Choose chicken breast over sliced chicken ham containing 70% meat, for example.)

Calories, fibre and yoghurt

Calories are simply the measure of energy contained in our food. They are a key concept in the next chapter! Fibre is important for a healthy digestive system. 'Live' yoghurt is also good, but keep to the low fat and low sugar varieties.

Vitamins and minerals

Your regular diet should supply you with all the nutrients you need, but when you are away from home you may need to take supplements. The more whole the food, the better it is. (Choose an orange in preference to orange juice in preference to a vitamin C tablet!)

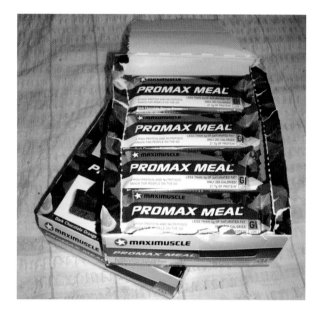

Obviously the amount you eat depends on how windy the regatta is, and how much water you personally are losing. The windier it is, the more fuel your body needs. Carbohydrates are the most readily converted to glycogen, the fuel of your muscles. Drink lots of water, even on a cold day, so urine remains 'pale and plentiful'.

15.2 What We Need to Eat

Remember, we are what we eat! Our bodies are constantly being rebuilt with the food we eat. High quality food (freshly produced, immediately frozen and with little or no processing) will make it easier to stay in optimum health. If you are feeling tired, one of

the main reasons may be poor diet. Unfortunately, when we get busy, not eating properly (followed by not sleeping properly) is often one of the consequences. Ultimately, this will be detrimental to our performance.

Timing is important. Do not eat 'heavy' meals immediately before sleep or exercise, as energy is then needed for our digestive system instead of for hiking or repairing. After a heavy meal we often feel tired because our bodies are concentrating on digesting food. If you get up and walk around you soon wake up, as your body realises it needs to do something else. Food should be eaten little and often, so there is room in the stomach for the food to churn and a constant supply of fuel and nutrients to the body.

Variety is the spice of life and food should be colourful (for example, a salad containing green, red and orange). Very heavily processed food may be white (white sugar as opposed to unrefined sugar) or unnatural in colour (bright orange or pink).

This is true of all food groups. A diet based purely on bread will not be as healthy as one which takes its carbohydrates from a variety of sources.

15.3 Diet Suggestions

In order to stick to a good, healthy diet we need to enjoy what we eat! Suddenly changing your diet may lead to an unhappy sailor – and unhappy sailors never tend to sail very well.

When you attend a regatta far from home, the food may be very different from what you are used to. Perhaps try and go out early so you can get used to the food, or bring some of your own if possible. In some foreign countries it is best to drink bottled water (safer than tap water). Remember, ice is simply frozen water. Even if the water is perfectly safe to drink, the fact that it is different from what your body is used to may affect your performance.

Saturday – Registration and rest day

9:00 Porridge for breakfast with 500ml water. Rigged boat
12:00 Chicken salad sandwich with 500ml water. Measure and enter
15:00 Tuna jacket potato and salad with 500ml water. Read sailing instructions, view weather and tidal data
18:00 Pasta bake and vegetables with 500ml water followed by early night.

Sunday – First day of racing, very windy

8:30 Porridge for breakfast with orange juice
10:30 A couple of bananas before launching
11:00 Race 1 followed by 500ml carbohydrate drink (8 grams of carbohydrate per 100ml fluid)
12:00 Race 2 followed by 500ml carbohydrate drink (8 grams of carbohydrate per 100ml fluid)
13:00 Race 3 followed by 500ml carbohydrate drink (8 grams of carbohydrate per 100ml fluid)
15:00 Return ashore for light pasta meal with 500ml water
18:00 Chicken breast, new potatoes and lots of vegetables. 500ml water
20:00 Ham and salad sandwich with 500ml water

Monday – Second day of racing, medium winds

8:30 Toast and jam for breakfast with orange juice
10:30 An energy bar before launching and 500ml water
11:00 Race 4 followed by an energy bar and 500ml water
12:00 Race 5 followed by an energy bar and 500ml water
13:00 Race 6 followed by an energy bar and 500ml water
15:00 Return ashore for ham and salad sandwich, 500ml water
18:00 Chicken risotto and 500ml water

Tuesday - Third day of racing, medium winds

8:30 Two bowls of wholegrain cereal with orange juice
10:30 A couple of apples
11:00 Race 7 followed by a 500ml carbohydrate drink (6.5 grams of carbohydrate per 100ml fluid)
12:00 Race 8 followed by a 500ml carbohydrate drink (6.5 grams of carbohydrate per 100ml fluid)
13:00 Race 9 followed by a 500ml carbohydrate drink (6.5 grams of carbohydrate per 100ml of fluid)
15:00 Return ashore for chicken and salad sandwich and 500ml water
18:00 Large jacket potato with tuna plus lots of salad and 500ml water.

Wednesday – fourth day of racing, light winds and hot

8:30 Porridge for breakfast with 500ml water
10:00 A tuna salad sandwich with 500 ml water
11:00 Race 10 followed by a carbohydrate drink (5 grams of carbohydrate per 100ml fluid)
12:00 Race 11 followed by a carbohydrate drink (5 grams of carbohydrate per 100ml fluid)
13:00 Race 12 followed by a carbohydrate drink (5 grams of carbohydrate per 100ml fluid)
15:00 Return ashore for tuna salad sandwich and 500ml water
18:00 Couscous with chicken salad and 500ml water

Thursday – fifth day of racing, strong winds

8:30 Porridge for breakfast with orange juice
11:00 Race 13 followed by 500ml carbohydrate drink (8 grams of carbohydrate per 100ml fluid)
12:00 Race 14 followed by 500ml carbohydrate drink (8 grams of carbohydrate per 100ml fluid)
14:00 Return ashore for large spaghetti Bolognaise and 500ml water
19:00 White fish with new potatoes plus lots of vegetables and 500ml water

Friday – sixth day of racing, medium winds

9:30 Porridge for breakfast with orange juice plus 500ml water
11:00 Race 15 followed by 500ml carbohydrate drink (5 grams of carbohydrate per 100ml fluid)
13:00 Tuna baguette with salad with 500ml water, then pack boat
17:00 Prize giving buffet then drive home.

Example of a Food diary

Advice from Joe Glanfield:

Sailors should always try to match the boat they sail to their natural size. This makes life a lot easier! I think what people eat and drink during a championship is a huge deal and still not fully valued enough in sailing. As sailors we race day in day out for a week for long hours, and it is hard to maintain the same level of concentration from day one to the last day of the championship. I think hydration is where most people go wrong, simply by not drinking enough of the right drinks during the day. I try and avoid alcohol and caffeine whilst competing, especially at a hot venue, and I often drink 5–7 litres of hydrating drink during the day.

Once when I was sailing in Melbourne I weighed myself before and after sailing. I had lost 3 kilograms. The next day I felt really low on energy. Since then I have been much more careful about the amount I drink whilst on the water.

Body Weight

Maintaining Body Weight and Recovering

Losing Body Weight

Gaining Body Weight

Advice from Joe Glanfield

16.1 Maintaining Body Weight and Recovering

The golden rule: In (food eaten) – Out (energy expended) = Accumulation (positive value gain fat, negative value lose fat). This simply means that if you eat 'too much' you get fat, and if you do not eat enough you get skinny (which does not equate to healthy!).

Yo-yo dieting is a big NO-NO. It is very unhealthy to keep gaining and losing body weight. Any change needs to be gradual and balanced (see Chapter 15) and be maintained. (This does not mean cutting out carbohydrates completely, or fat or proteins…)

The issue with yo-yo dieting is that it sends mixed messages to your body. When you cut calories the metabolism will often slow down, and the body may even go into starvation mode. So, when food is taken on, it is more likely to be stored as fat (because the body is preparing for its next fast!). Women who diet constantly will, in later life,

Use a good set of scales.

tend to form a pear shape because weight is lost from the top first and gained on the bottom first. Men will develop a beer belly because this is where fat accumulates first in males and is the last place for it to be lost. It means that there may be fatty deposits around the internal organs, which is obviously not desirable.

With either weight loss or weight gain it may be necessary to take some time away from sailing so you can concentrate on getting to the desired weight as soon as possible. (Allow more time for weight training for weight gain or running for weight loss).

When you are out on the race course it is too late to adjust body weight. Do not try and starve/force feed yourself just before you go out on the water. If anything, it is probably best to forget about it, or perhaps try some mental imagery. (Imagine yourself heavy on windy days and light on light days).

16.2 Losing Body Weight

First consider if you can maintain the target weight with a healthy diet. If you can, you need to lose calories by reducing calorie intake (still stick to the healthy percentages but eat less food) and increasing calorie expenditure by doing more exercise.

One of the healthiest ways to decrease body fat (while maintaining all your muscle mass) is to increase the amount of aerobic activity. This can be pretty much anything. Running is perhaps the easiest to do, as it just requires a good pair of trainers, but has the highest impact. Most modern gyms come with a good range of equipment, so you really can take your pick of machines. Just check the heart rate is high enough (using a heart-rate monitor). You should aim to train at around 60% of your maximum heart rate (which is approximately 220 – your age) to get a good combination of fitness and fat burning.

To lose 1 kg of body fat requires around 7500 fewer calories. This means that most people should not aim to lose more than 1

or 2 kgs per week (a calories deficit of around 500–1000 a day). The more rapid the weight loss, the more likely it is that lean tissue may be lost (which means a loss in strength). Also, the more restrictive a diet is in terms of total calories, the harder it is to maintain a healthy diet.

Sudden weight loss is not recommended, but it may be desirable for classes where a weigh-in is required. This way the crew can, for example, weigh a kilogram or so more each, drop this weight for the weigh-in and then replace it. The healthiest way to do this is to lose the fluid as close as possible to the weigh-in and then replace it straight after. Increasing potassium levels (citrus fruits are high in potassium) can help to excrete water, and vigorous exercise will help sweat the weight out. After weigh-in, drink to recover the weight as soon as possible. Ideally, take a hypotonic drink with electrolytes so the drink is absorbed quicker and retained longer, providing maximum rehydration. Short-term fasting is not recommended.

16.3 Gaining Body Weight

Additional weight should come from muscle. Being stronger has additional benefits: you can lift heavier sheet loads more easily. Increasing body fat means that you have to carry all that weight around without the additional strength to do so. You should aim to maximise the lean tissue weight gain. This means combining a healthy diet (see Chapter 15) with exercise (see Chapter 14). Aiming for a maximum of around 0.5–1 kg of lean tissue per week would require an additional 500–1000 extra calories per day.

A weight-training programme to gain weight means little rest and lots of sets of the compound exercises – those involving several muscle groups (squat, deadlift, chin-ups, shoulder and chest press) – for around 10 repetitions for on your own) each time with the help of a spotter. Be prepared for some muscle soreness 24 hours later. (DOMS – delayed onset muscle soreness – shows you have been working hard.) Do not start such a programme if you are not an experienced trainer. If you have never been in a gym, start with a normal fitness programme.

Being the right body weight makes boat handling much easier.

Advice from Joe Glanfield:

I think that knowing your body weight and keeping it consistent is important. If you're always putting on weight and then crash dieting, you don't get used to sailing at a certain weight, and in some classes your weight heavily affects the rig you use. Personally, I would always rather be in the middle of the weight range used in the class. You can then forget about it and concentrate on more important things.

Nick and I try and change body weight if we know an event is going to be in particularly light or strong winds, but only by a small amount and over a long period of time.

Mental Attitude

The Importance of Correct Attitude

Dealing with Negatives

Relaxation Techniques

Advice from Joe Glanfield

17.1 The Importance of Correct Attitude

In order to win, you not only need to be physically fit but mentally fit. There is no point preparing your body to win if you do not prepare your mind! At the top level of sailing, championships are won and lost on mental skills more than physical skills. Mental fitness can take as long, if not longer, to achieve than physical fitness.

Quite simply – you must have a positive attitude at all times. Think of it this way: positive thinking brings positive results (and negative thinking brings negative results). This occurs in many areas of life, not just in the sport of sailing. Putting yourself in high-pressure situations, as soon and as often as possible, helps you to deal with the pressure. This is why attending a warm-up event prior to a major championship can be so beneficial.

Before you start looking into your various goals (perhaps this chapter should have been at the beginning of the book!), you need to decide whether you have the commitment and determination to see the goal through to the end. If your goal is simply to succeed at club level (using your own definition of success), the mental skills required will be less than to win an Olympic medal. Having said that, lack of mental skills can still hold you back.

Increased pressure can bring anxiety, which can only have a detrimental effect on your racing. This is especially noticeable in those new to the sport with limited race experience. This is why attending lots of stressful regattas is a good thing! However, pick your regattas carefully. If you end up doing too many regattas back to back the pressure can cause you to burn out. Careful planning is important. As you get older you learn what brings out the best in you.

Pressure affects people in different ways, and people handle it differently. (There are some useful techniques to help deal with anxiety and aggression in the last part of this chapter.) Some people do not handle pressure well. Try and keep away from them whilst racing, as their attitude could rub off on you. Try and be professional at all times and give yourself the best possible chance of winning. As soon as you think you cannot win, you have made it more or less impossible to do so.

Aggression is, of course, the other trait that comes with high-pressure situations. Controlled aggression can be very useful; it can help you hike harder and for longer, get the spinnaker down quicker, etc. However, uncontrolled aggression could cause you to get involved in silly incidents, or even protested under rule 69 (gross misconduct).

Your natural demeanour will play a role: you cannot change who you are. From this perspective, some people may be better suited to multi-crewed boats than others. Remember, your attitude can – and most often will – affect those around you. Talk to those near you so they know your feelings. If you shout and swear you may be seen to

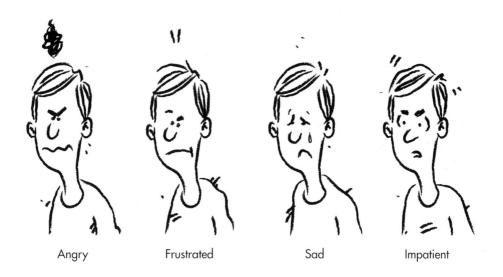

Angry   Frustrated   Sad   Impatient

have a bad attitude, but if you are very quiet people may think you do not care about racing performance.

17.2 Dealing with Negatives

Often it is more what you do about handling the lows, rather than how you handle the highs that affects performance. How do you refocus as quickly as possible? If you are campaigning on your own this can be especially difficult without other people to help you. A close friend, girl/boyfriend, husband/wife may be the ideal person to help elevate your mood, or you may find it better to work it through on your own. Experience is important here, and sometimes you may find out what not to do (to improve your mood) first.

There are so many variables in sailing, most of which are completely beyond your control. Often you may feel the weather (wind, waves, current, etc.) is conspiring against you. However, over time, the law of averages says things will go your way: you just have to stick with it.

Often the best way to deal with negatives is just to consider the positives. However small they are, you must have done something right at some point! What are your strengths? Think about these rather than your weaknesses, or what has just gone wrong.

When things are going really well it may be time to take a small break, as you do not want to get to the point where you overtrain. You should not wait until you do not want to train/cannot train before you stop! This applies to the short and the long term. You should always feel you want to do more sailing.

There are two real steps to dealing with the negatives: focus on a positive (one of your perceived strengths) or try and forget about the negative emotion and use a relaxation technique which works for you. Negative thoughts and feelings manifest themselves physically, and so the sooner they are resolved the better.

Whatever you do, do not make excuses as to why it was acceptable to lose the places, make the mistakes, etc. Accept what has happened and move on as soon as you can. You can only affect situations which are going to happen; what has happened can never be changed.

17.3 Relaxation Techniques

Many of the top sailors in the world use relaxation techniques, perhaps without even being aware they are doing so. They vary from the simple – taking 10 deep (belly) breaths, which has a physiological calming effect (if the body is calm it is easier for the mind to follow) – to techniques that require a bit of practice. Different people require different things. Simply having a key word (such as focus or concentrate) can be enough to get things back on track.

Detachment and Mental Imagery

Try and detach yourself from the situation. Think of a good (positive) time when you were relaxed and happy; remember it in as much detail as possible. The sounds, smells, colours, tastes and textures will all help to make the experience become more believable. The scene could be a desert island, a spring meadow or a running waterfall. Just something to remove the stress you are currently under.

Reframe

Perhaps it would be better just to change the focus. Often the main cause of frustration is factors beyond our control. Start focusing on the factors that you can control. Keep the boat flat, for example. Now go through the processes: hike hard or go as low as possible on the trapeze. Really concentrate on the sheet and/or steering (depending upon your role). Now when the boat is up to speed you can start considering your options…

Keywords

These remove negative feelings and the effect they have on performance. A simple key word may be enough for some people. The most common are 'relax' or 'breathe', but it can be anything that takes your thoughts away from the immediate issue. Usually the word will be related to either a feeling or a state, and it can be 'shouted' in your head or written on your boom.

Pattern Breaking

Distract yourself from negative thoughts and feelings by taking the energy away from the negative thinking. Maybe pinch yourself, say a key word, or simply hike a bit harder. Now think about your affirmations.

Affirmations

They must be positive sentences that describe the way you want to be. They should focus upon a specific aspect of your performance: 'I am always fast in strong winds.' They need to be personal (I), positive (what you want) and present ('am' not 'will be').

Rational Analysis and Relaxation

Off the water you need think about your beliefs and how they can affect your performance. Irrational barriers can limit performance. Take Roger Bannister for example, the first person to break the 4-minute mile. There is no reason why the step up from 4 minutes 1 second to 4 dead should be any more difficult than 4 minutes dead to 3 minutes 59 seconds, but there was an irrational barrier which said a mile could not be run in less than 4 minutes. Rational analysis challenges you to think differently.

Relaxation is vital in sailing. There are so many factors beyond your control it is important to find time to relax after racing. Simply find a quiet place and a comfortable position (sitting or lying down), focus on your breathing, and allow a minimum of two or three minutes to relax your whole body.

Advice from Joe Glanfield:

I have noticed that there is one trait that is common to all the very best Olympic sailors: they are very reluctant to ever use an excuse, or say they were 'unlucky'. If you think about it, sailing is all about managing luck and risk. If you say you were unlucky in a race, it means you cannot learn from it, or practise it the next time you train. If you say it was a mistake, you can learn from it and find a reason for it.

If you want to be the best at sailing you need to banish all excuses. If someone beats you, accept they must have been better, learn why, and then try and beat them next time.

I believe arousal control is an essential part of any sailor's mental preparation. There is a huge difference between racing in strong winds and racing in light winds. When you are preparing for a strong-wind race it is more physical and things are happening quickly, so hype yourself up before you launch and make sure you are feeling on edge and alert. (A rugby or football player would do something similar.). In light winds, however, you need to make gentle, precise movements and you have time to make decisions on the tactics, so you need to calm yourself before you launch and focus (like a chess or snooker player).

Racing Log

Why Keep a Diary?

How to Keep Good Records

Race Analysis

Advice from Joe Glanfield

18.1 Why Keep a Diary?

The key reason for keeping a diary is to show where you are. This can help you get to where you want to be. In terms of motivation it can be very useful to see all your hard work paying off! Weeks, months and even years later, you can use it to see where you came from and how far you have progressed.

It is easy to quantify some aspects of sailing: your body weight, the distance and time you ran, the weights you lifted. This shows you where you are and can also help you realise how long it is going to take you to get to where you want to be.

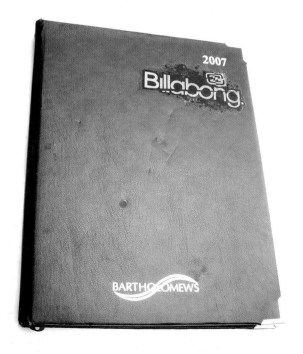

Some aspects of sailing are much harder to quantify, such as the feeling of going fast in a certain condition. In a way, these aspects are even more important to record as they are easier to forget (as opposed to, well, I usually bench press around XX kgs).

Logging the number of hours you train can also be reassuring when you come to do a regatta, as you know you have put the time in. Alternatively, if you have not been putting in the time your log will show this, hopefully enabling you to identify the problem sooner rather than later. Try and be as precise as possible. Record the actual time spent on the water and do not include the time spent in the boat park.

One of the biggest differences between amateur and professional sailors is the time on the water. This helps you develop a natural feel. You may be able to keep the boat going in very light or very strong winds just as fast as someone who has spent 10 times as much time in the boat as you have – for a couple of minutes. But it will require all your concentration, whereas it will be much more natural for them, and so they will be able to keep 'in the groove' (sheeting and steering accurately) for far longer. This is why time on the water is so important. In easy-to-sail conditions (say

8 knots and flat water) the differences in boats across the fleet are noticeably smaller.

Keeping careful track of issues outside of sailing is also useful so that stray thoughts do not encroach on you whilst racing (oh, I need to buy a chicken for dinner as the in-laws are coming over...).

18.2 How to Keep Good Records

What works for one person may not work for another, but the key thing is to record as much information as possible, as consistently as possible, so it can be easily accessed in the future.

Any measurements need to be specified as clearly as you can (weight on the bathroom scales, having been to the loo, at 8:00; length from the top of the mast to the centre of the back of the boat, etc.).

Hardback books are usually better than loose sheets of paper; you are less likely to lose them and they last far longer.

Remember RAP record:

Relevant: Record the things which can and do change, and do so in a way that makes it easy to make comparisons at a later date.

Accurate: Make sure what you are writing is correct, not what you think is correct! Is it 68 kgs, or have the scales not been properly reset?

Precise: Pay attention to detail. Is it actually 67.5 kgs?

It is always a good idea to record things as soon as possible, so you do not forget them or misremember them. Wet Notes (paper and pens which can be used on the water) can be very useful. You can then transfer your data to your racing log after sailing.

WEIGHT TRAINING PROGRAMME

MAXIMUSCLE
Sports nutrition at its best

Training with Professionals

Date 8/2/08   Bodypart(s)   LEGS
Workout duration 90 MINS   Day: LEGS (DAY FOUR)

Exercise	Set 1	Set 2	Set 3	Set 4	Set 5	Set 6	Set 7
SQUAT	60	60	80	80	100	100	120
	15	15	12	12	10	10	8
DEAD LIFT	80	80	80	120	120	120	
	15	15	15	10	10	10	
LUNGE	50	50	50				
	10	10	10				
LEG. EXT.	60	60	60				
	12	12	12				
LEG. CURL.	60	60	60				
	12	12	12				
CALF RAISE	80	80	80				
	20	20	20				

18.2a Weight training diary.

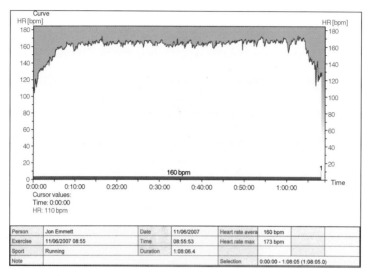

18.2b Heart rate graph on computer.

Date	9/2/08
Time	11:00 to 15:00
Venue	Portland Harbour
Wind speed	Mean 16 knots, gusts 20 knots, lulls 12 knots
Wind direction	240 +/– 10
Waves	0.3 metres
Sails	Training sails: Jib 4, Main 3, Spinnaker 4
Jib Track	Hole 3
Jib clew	Hole 3
Lower mast bend	20 mm
Shroud tension	29
Cap tension	15
Comment	Good height, slightly overpowered in the gusts.

18.2c Rig tuning diary.

18.3 Race Analysis

Even after the most difficult race, you should debrief yourself. There are always some positives to come from the way you sailed. Just remember, mistakes should be treated as learning opportunities. Do not beat yourself up about what went wrong, but instead work out how you could improve things next time.

If you are lucky enough to have coaches for training sessions or regattas, try and get them to make some notes and give these to you afterwards.

You should take the time to consider the day's racing/training on the same day, when thoughts and feelings are still fresh, even if you are a bit emotionally charged. Putting things off to another day is never the best solution. (Although sometimes it may be good practice to have a second look at things a bit later).

There are some venues where you will be racing many times in your sailing career. Try and extract your notes and produce a little venue guide (not only about the racing, but also

where you liked to stay, eat, the easiest way to get there, etc.). Quantify things where you can, and make sure you use the same anemometer and compass for all your wind readings.

Advice from Joe Glanfield:

How much you write depends on the person and the circumstances. If you have a lot of things going on outside of sailing, you will find that you forget things quicker and need to write more down. I think it is very important to keep a track of the settings you used in racing, as it stops you going in circles and making the same mistakes twice.

I like to keep a log of the number of hours I have sailed in different conditions. If there is an imbalance, I can correct this by focusing my training on the conditions I have sailed in less.

I think it is really important to write your goals down – not just your overall performance goal, but also your goals for each training session. Somehow writing them down makes you commit to them more; it also means you can look back at them after a while and see what you were trying to achieve at different times in the year.

Concentration

Looking at Mental Stamina

Maintaining Focus

Peak Concentration

Advice from Joe Glanfield

19.1   Looking at Mental Stamina

When things are really tough, can you keep going? Or do you let frustration get the better of you? Remember sleep and diet are not just important for your physical well-being; they help your mental state as well. Sailing is a sport where often it pays to be patient. This can be hard if you have not had enough sleep or have eaten poorly (or especially if you are dehydrated).

You need to train according to how you expect to race. If you are doing three one-hour races a day, then your typical training session should be three and a half hours. Make sure you have enough food and water for this time and ensure that you are working just as hard as if it were a real race. As soon as you start thinking, 'It doesn't matter, it is only training, the quality of the session is lost.

Training on your own is a great way to build mental stamina, as it is always easier to work hard to sail fast when you have someone else to beat. Training on your own can make you really think about the way you sail without the outside influence of someone else. This also means you can get some training that those you may be racing against do not have.

If possible, try and work with different people as everyone has different skills. See how they deal with difficult situations, as you may find a solution that will work for you.

- Do you find it easier to get to the boat park early, rig, and then go and find a quiet area?

- Or do you get to the boat park at the same time as most people, but plug in and listen to some music?

- Or do you arrive with just enough time to rig and launch immediately? (Some people will require more or less time on the race course to get familiar with the conditions.)

Consider which approach will leave you the most mentally fit and best prepared. You may find that a different approach will work on different days. For example, if you are racing in the afternoon, having a light pasta lunch and then going to the boat park may work best, but if you are morning racing you may choose to rig and then have breakfast.

Some people find that their mental and physical states affect their eating patterns. Some may find that eating will help settle the nerves (and the stomach) and prevent stomach cramps. Others will not feel like eating, so they need to eat breakfast earlier than normal as the stress may slow their digestion. However you react, try not to worry about it; just look back in your racing log to see what works best for you (eating normally, eating early, just taking energy drinks).

1. Over tired
2. Not enjoying racing/training
3. Don't care about result/distracters
4. Feeling under pressure to perform
5. Nervous (may have related tummy issues)

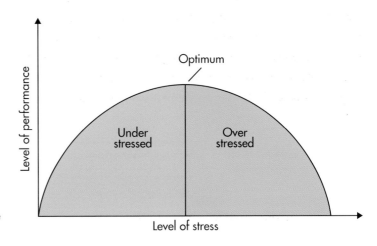

19.1a
Factors that can decrease mental energies.

Often regattas are sailed with several races over several days, which can be really hard, and it is not unusual to feel completely mentally drained. Try experimenting with the best way to relax and get this energy back: reading, watching TV, chatting to friends, going to the cinema. However if you cannot maintain concentration you need to refocus as soon as possible (see below).

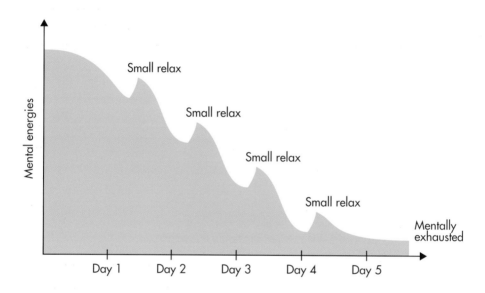

19.1b Showing mental fatigue over time.

Finding a routine (wake up time, eating time, bedtime) can really help the concentration in a regatta. Because lots of decisions have already been made for each day it saves you from having to do too much thinking.

Mental skills do come with age, which is why sailing rewards experience so much. Young sailors need to do as much sailing as possible, to improve mental fitness as well as physical fitness. The ability to concentrate under pressure is vital if you are going to be successful. Often more can be learned from a failure than a success, providing a turning point and motivation to go further.

19.2 Maintaining Focus

How do you refocus? Well, this depends largely upon the individual. If the issue is acute then there are lots of techniques to help you get your head back in the race. Some of these are listed below. However, if the problem is chronic, taking some time away from the sport may be required. This is more often a problem for those who are full-time sailing, (who should have some other interests in their lives to keep the motivation high), but it can happen to young sailors who have done little sailing during school time and then find themselves on the water every day over the summer. Remember, both training and racing need to be fun. If you are not enjoying yourself it is harder to push yourself to do well.

The sooner you can refocus the better. This may require the presence of someone else (perhaps a more experienced sailor) to ask some questions to get you talking, perhaps to resolve the issue or even to help you try and forget about it. (Ask questions such as 'what is for dinner?') However, if you are on your own you may need to work the issue out yourself. Try some of the techniques given in Chapter 17.

When racing you need to be focusing on the right thing at the right time. The majority of the time this may be boat speed. However, near marks or where boats are close together, boat-to-boat tactics and boat handling become important.

The boat speed required may vary: it may be important to go high (trim the boat flat and set the sails flat with a tight leach) or fast (some heel, fuller sails, more twist in the sail). The focus is very different in both, and communication between the crew is vital.

There are four different types of concentration (see figure 19.2a):

1. Narrow external – focusing on one or two areas outside the boat, for example the wind on the water and the waves.

2. Broad external – assessing a large changing situation – most of the fleet are going right.

3. Narrow internal – focusing on one or more areas inside the boat – the actions to perform a boat handling manoeuvre.

4. Broad internal – assessing your boat to boat tactics.

Here the width (narrow to broad), gives the close focus or the big picture, and the direction (internal or external), focuses inside or outside your boat.

Most people will tend towards one type of concentration and it is sometimes difficult to get your head out of the boat (2+4) when you are worried about getting the telltales flying (3), or you may find you are worried about the boats around you (2+4) when you should be concentrating on boat speed (1+3). In a crewed boat you can of course share the responsibilities. The most important thing to switch on/off is when to concentrate 100% on boat speed as shown in figure 19.2 b.

The focus outside the boat can also change: are you looking for a flat patch of water (either for boat speed or to find somewhere to tack or gybe)? Or pressure? Or angle of wind? Which is the most important thing to look for?

To make it easier to concentrate on the most important things, write them down (on waterproof paper) so you can refer to them if and when needed. This information can

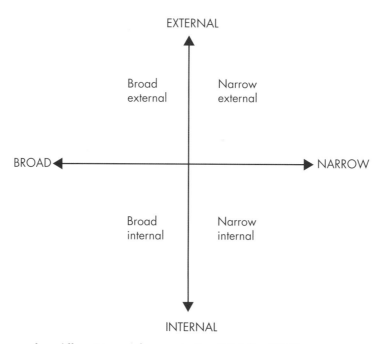

19.2a There are four different types of concentration (Nideffer 1976).

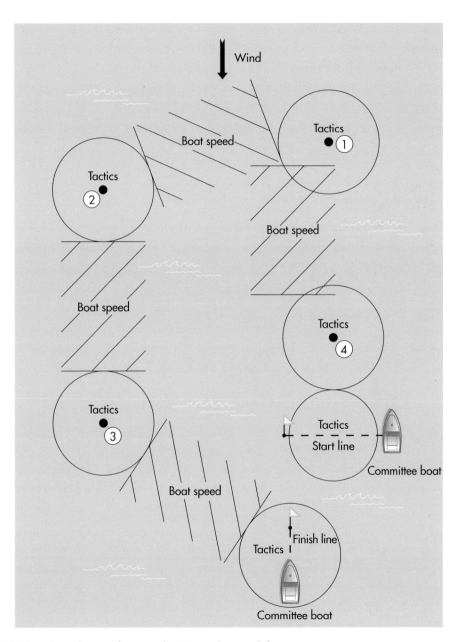

19.2b Showing where to focus on boat speed around the race course.

include your group (if not racing as one fleet), your start time, the course, the weather and current predictions and your preferred rig setting. It does not matter if you do not need the information, but at least you have it for peace of mind.

Regularly check that the information is as accurate and up-to-date as possible, and also readable. (If the information has been written on your boat, it could get rubbed off. The paper it has been written on could start to fall apart. If laminated, the tape holding it on could start to pull off.)

19.3   Peak Concentration

It is impossible to sail at your very best every hour of every day, every day of every week, every week of every year and every year of your life! You therefore need to consider the most important time(s) for you to peak and how long it will take. Remember the different elements, such as boat work (see Chapter 20) and fitness (see Chapter 14).

However, the moment you are most focused is when the subconscious takes over. This is sometimes referred to as 'being in the zone'. You almost feel as if you have woken up to find that you have sailed very fast and moved away from boats around you.

When you try REALLY hard to concentrate you can make things worse, as you do not relax enough to feel the boat, and you can easily get frustrated if you fall out of phase with the wind and the waves.

Unfortunately, it is not possible to just put yourself in the zone. All you can do is lots of racing until you know what to do and can relax, switch off and almost steer/ sheet/trim by instinct. This is why mental fitness is such a vital part of successful sailing. Being in the zone just happens naturally.

If you cannot relax and get in the zone, try not to let this worry you, as this way you will never get there! Instead, try and concentrate on the most important variable (perhaps spotting the shifts). When you are happy with this, try and take on more variables, while still paying attention to the first (and most important one). You may find that, with time, you can concentrate on the first variable without trying.

Advice from Joe Glanfield:

The key to sailing is remembering that you can't fully concentrate on every variable all the time: there are simply too many. What makes good sailors really good is the ability to pick the variables that need the most concentration for a certain course or condition and block out the ones that won't make much difference.

Remember, hydration has a huge effect on concentration and is really important if you want to be able to concentrate for long days every day. If I am sailing in hot weather I usually wear a hat, and I am sure it helps me maintain concentration.

I have a fairly strict routine before I launch for a race, in terms of what time I get down to the sailing club, the order I do things and how much I will let myself think and talk about anything other than the race coming up. All of this helps to make sure that when you launch you are in 'race mode' immediately and concentrate to the best of your ability.

Looking at the results before racing can make your mind concentrate on the wrong things just before you launch. I do look at the results during an event, but normally only in the evening so they are not on my mind just before I launch.

If I am at a high-pressure event and there are a lot of distractions at the sailing club, wearing headphones and listening to music is a really good way to block out things going on whilst I'm getting the boat ready.

Boat Preparation

How Prepared is Your Boat?

Dealing with Boat Work

Checklist

Advice from Simon Hiscocks

20.1 How Prepared is Your Boat?

You need a fast and well-prepared boat in order to win! You should care for and maintain your boat: there is rarely an excuse for gear failure. Examine the class rules carefully and make sure you take advantage of any possible improvements you can make (reducing weight, making control systems easy to operate) but stay in class! You certainly do not want a disqualification for being out of class.

In a nutshell you need to be racing with:

- the lightest, stiffest and smoothest hull;
- the best spars, sails and foils for the prevailing conditions (these may be relative to your bodyweight); and
- easy-to-operate control systems in an effective layout.

Wash the boat so it is clean and dry. Make any repairs and polish once every 100 days. Boats do have a limited life, but you can extend this by storing them carefully and trailing them conscientiously. Make preparations to replace a hull before it is worn out (in case there are any delays in getting the replacement boat!).

Foils should be sanded and may be polished. Use a coarse paper and work down (for example, 400, 800, 1200, 1600 grit). Finish with some fine rubbing compound. You can minimise the wear to foils, hulls AND spars by keeping them covered up as much as possible.

Spars do break, so it is vital to have a spare set for which you know the

measurements. If you find spars you like (and can afford to do so), buy two with the same measurements.

What is good for one person is not necessarily good for another. You need to minimise the friction in a system, and get the compromise between the amount of rope you have to pull on and how hard it is to pull. Be especially careful to make sure you can get the maximum and minimum settings without a system bottoming out (when two

blocks touch and prevent further movement).

You may well have to do lots of testing to decide which gear you want to use. If you do not have this time, you may be better using kit you are used to and can train with regularly. It is rarely a good idea to start using new kit just before a championship.

If you are chartering, get to the venue early and get familiar with the boat you will be racing. You could take your own customised bits and pieces.

Even in one-design boats there are small differences in equipment. If possible (time and budget?) obtain several masts and sails and test them to find a favourite. You may need to pool resources with people at your local club, allowing the heaviest sailor the stiffest mast and fullest sail, etc…

Common mistakes

- Allowing foils/hull/spars to become scratched by dropping, etc. Always use padding/covers when transporting. If you need to make a quick repair, always use Plastic Padding or some other material that is softer than the gel coat, so you can sand it away easily. Many fillers require a minimum temperature, so try and get this temperature (do the work indoors, or on a warm day). Remember, too cold or too hot can be equally bad news. It may be worth investing in a small fan heater for long trips away.

- Allowing foils/spars/sails to be overexposed to the sun causes them to bend (foils), fatigue early (carbon spars) or shrink (sails). Regularly check any joins (spars will often fail around the rivets) and areas of high load (the spinnaker stitching, the head, tack and clew of sails) as these are the points which are likely to fail.

20.2 Dealing with Boat Work

Before you even start boat work you need to decide the most efficient way (both in terms of cost and time) of dealing with the issue. Would it be better to pay a professional to do the work (for example, structural repairs), while you spend a day raising funds for your campaign? Or is it a skill you need to develop so you can make changes quickly during a regatta (for example, splicing lines)?

Although it may pay to divide the boat work within the team so people work on the areas they excel at, it is good practice if everyone is able to do every task. This way, if one crew member is unable to work (though sickness, injury, etc.) the job can

Thoroughly clean your boat from bow to stern.

still get done. (This means that in a single-handed boat you definitely need to be able to do everything!)

If at all possible, allow more time than you think is required. In a regatta situation it can be easy to become distracted, or it may be harder to get the items you need. Good boat work may not win regattas, but bad work can certainly stop you winning.

Now polish your clean boat.

20.3   Checklist

It is not only when preparing yourself that making checklists can pay dividends. Boat preparation should start as early as possible. Often the most time-effective method is to check everything when the boat comes off the water. This allows you the maximum amount of time to rectify any problems and/or order any parts needed. If parts need to be replaced frequently, it would be well worth ordering two at a time (rolls of electrical (insulation) tape, for example, could be bought 10 at a time!).

When you get a new boat (depending upon the class), there may well be over a week's worth of boat work to do! When you first buy a new boat write down everything you do. As you own more boats of the same class you will find you can refine this list.

If you charter a boat or buy one second-hand, it is a good idea to use the 'new boat checklist' to go over what needs to be done. When you sell a boat, it is nice to pass on a checklist to the new owner so they do not have any nasty surprises in six months, when something wears out through normal wear and tear. Generally, you find the higher the performance of the boat, the more boat work there is!

'The best prepared will win' is an old sporting maxim, and when it comes to sailing it is only too true. Of course, there are many areas of boat preparation but each must be addressed equally for a complete performance. Although hours can be spent, or even wasted, on boat preparation, a lack of attention in this area will be blatantly obvious, as the boat will break.

Think of boat preparation in terms of levels. The basic level is fundamental to anyone, an ability to get around the course without anything breaking, or parts falling off. Beyond that levels range from having competitive kit and efficient systems to having the best possible hull finish and the lightest possible equipment for an Olympic or America's Cup competitor.

Once your level is achieved, there are a number of factors that need to be considered. Does the boat comply with the class rules? Have its sails or boat parts been measured correctly? What will happen if something breaks, or (more accurately) needs replacing before it breaks? Do you need to carry spares? Do you have the tools to remove and replace those spares? There is little point in taking tools that either don't work or are not required. Most boats will need just a handful of tools to keep them running. For instance, a basic level of need for a 49er is a Phillips screwdriver, two 10-mm spanners, a knife, a lighter, a bit of wire or a splicing needle and some whipping twine. Spares, of course, could run to a spare boat, but this would not only be unpractical, but also not really financially viable. In most cases, spares are more important than tools, particularly if they are to hand and ready to be used.

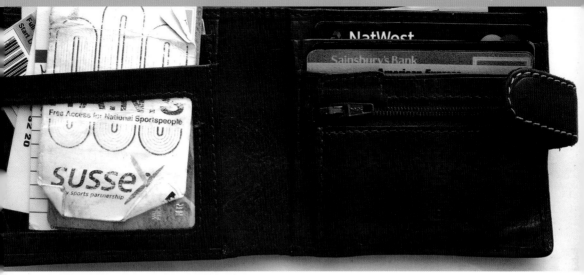

Finance

The True Cost of Sailing

Campaigning

Sponsorship

Advice from Joe Glanfield

21.1 The True Cost of Sailing

Competing in any sport at the top level is not cheap. In order to be competitive there is a minimum spend, which will vary considerably depending upon the boat being sailed. This is one of the first considerations you should address when looking into joining the class, as it may well be the limiting factor on your performance.

Having a coach support you every time you go on the water is the ideal situation, but far from most people's budget. Hence the reason for writing this book: to help people be their own coach. However, if you do have the money for a coach, consider carefully when is the most appropriate time to use him or her.

If finance is a major issue (which you should have realised from the beginning when you filled out your dartboard), you need to think how you are going to address this. Are you going to limit the number of regattas in your campaign? Train with old kit? Work more, or sail less? Try and find sponsorship? Or perhaps a combination of the above? You may even have to consider sailing a different class of boat, with one-design, low performance boats in the main being the cheapest option.

Having said this, money certainly does not buy success, especially in one-design boats. In fact, having lots of funds can be a distraction as the temptation to do too much (sailing, testing, racing) may be tempting, especially if you have previously been limited by your finances. However, having some money in reserve as a safety net can be very comforting in case the unthinkable happens!

If you are joining a class for the first time, speak to experienced campaigners. While they may not be specific, they will probably be able to give you a 'ballpark figure' of the minimum spend for a successful campaign. Just sit down and work out what you need, and then cost it up. Good second-hand equipment can often be bought for around 50% of the price of new, but this will, of course, be dependant upon availability. Speak to established teams who may be changing their kit regularly. (If you make a living from the sport, which is results dependant, you will always be wanting to have the best possible equipment. All other things being equal, new is always better than old.)

You may need to make several sacrifices (time and/or money) for your sailing. You need to ask yourself whether you are really prepared to do so. If the answer is yes, great. If not, you may need to reconsider the level you are aiming for. When you realise just how hard you had to work to get to the regatta, it can be a great motivator to perform as well as you can.

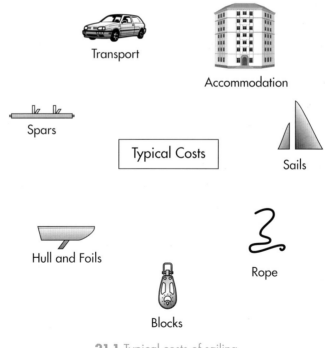

Transport

Accommodation

Spars

Typical Costs

Sails

Hull and Foils

Rope

Blocks

21.1 Typical costs of sailing

21.2 Campaigning

In order to be successful at an event you need a good build up: quality training, attending other regattas, testing kit and improving physical and mental fitness. Any champion will have paid attention to every aspect of a campaign (each chapter of this book), but depending upon the class and his/her relative experience, the sailor will have spent more time on some aspects than others.

Many campaigns extend over a number of years, and so the cost of one year may be widely different from the next, even if you do the same programme, as there are so many variable costs in sailing. The cost of materials or getting materials may change, as may logistic costs.

Once campaigning, you need to stick to your budget, however tight this is. Try not to let any financial concerns follow you onto the race course. This is easier said than done, but vital for your successful racing. Break the budget down so you know what the money is going on and try to budget for small units of time (like a month say), so if you start going over-budget you can address it quickly (or perhaps, if you have some money left over, you can order some new kit).

Where possible, it is always good to separate any campaign finances from your own personal ones (even if it is done only theoretically). This makes it easier to work out the true level of spending. Also, if the team splits, it makes things much easier if people own different parts of the campaign outright, thereby hopefully making any change of crew as amicable as possible. Items to consider:

An example of possible campaign costs

Sails	£1200	4 sets	£4800
Rope	£112	2 sets	£224
Blocks	£370	1 set	£370
Hull & Foils	£5750	1 set	£5750
Spars	£1800	3 sets	£5400
Logistics	£945	Mileage	£1520
	£475	Accommodation	

21.2a

Value of investment to campaign (ideal)

	New cost	Importance to campaign	Value added to campaign
Sails	4800	.7	£3360.00
Rope	224	.9	£201.60
Blocks	370	.5	£185.00
Hull & Foils	5750	.4 (will be .6 next year)	£2300.00
Spars	5400	.6	£3240.00
Logistics	1520	.8	£1216.00

21.2b Value of investment to a campaign

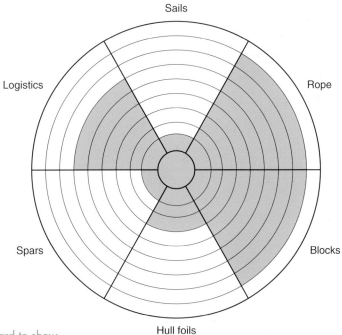

21.2c Dartboard to show spending priorities

When considering any investment, try and work out the possible benefit. Is a new sail more or less important than a day's coaching? Would a new boat be better than flying to Australia to do a couple of regattas? Cost out the various options and then multiply by the perceived value, which you rate from 0 to 1. Be careful to be honest with yourself. Lastly, check your campaign dartboard to ensure that you are not completely forgetting one aspect of your sailing.

21.3 Sponsorship

In most countries the profile of sailing as a sport has improved as the accessibility of the sport develops. Sailing is now seen as a good sport to be involved in, as it is both

---

Dear Sir/Madam (name is better),

Opening paragraph introducing yourself and giving details of sailor's background and request.

Key benefits of being a sponsor:

- Prime coverage on clothing, boat and vehicle
- Coverage on website
- Regular campaign reports
- Pictures and video from regattas
- Hospitality to suit the company's needs

List of regattas attending this year:

Regatta Name	Start Date	End Date	Venue
Tornado Asia Pacific Championships	2/1/08	9/1/08	Australia
Sail Melbourne International Regatta	14/1/08	19/1/08	Australia
Rolex Miami Olympic Classes Regatta	27/1/08	2/2/08	USA
Tornado World Championship	22/2/08	1/3/08	New Zealand
HRH Princess Sofia Trophy	15/3/08	21/3/08	Spain
Semaine Olympique Française	19/4/08	25/4/08	France
Tornado European Championships	2/5/08	10/5/08	Greece
Holland Regatta	21/5/08	25/5/08	Netherlands
Kieler Woche	21/6/08	29/6/08	Germany
Skandia Sail for Gold Regatta	17/9/08	21/9/08	Great Britain
Christmas Race	17/12/08	22/12/08	Spain

Final paragraph summarising key benefits to both parties.

Yours faithfully (if you use Sir/Madam),
Yours sincerely (if you know the name),

21.3 Typical sponsorship proposal.

258

technically and environmentally friendly, whilst having the normal sporting attributes of fitness and health. The downside is the profile (due to lack of media coverage, especially TV), which is not as good as for many other sports.

Sponsorship used to be a company doing something nice for a team. Now the role has almost reversed and it is a sailor doing something for the company (and getting some degree of support in return). Think of what unique opportunities you can offer and make any approach as professional as possible.

Remember that the value of goods which a company produces (such as cars, electronic equipment or sailing items) is far higher to you than their cost of producing them. So forming relationships to gain free rope, sails or whatever can make a real difference to your campaign, and you can offer the company feedback to help them improve their products and promote their brand.

Public speaking and hospitality are two of the greatest benefits that you can offer a company, but you need to practise, especially if you are not naturally an extrovert. Know your talk inside out, how long it takes and how best to deliver it. Do dummy runs for family and friends. If you repeat a talk, try and make it different – some of your audience may have heard it before!

Once you have obtained a sponsor, treat them well, keep talking to them and show you represent good value for money. Good sponsors tend to be harder to get than to keep. Having said this, always have a plan B in case your sponsorship falls through. This way you do not have to stop completely if your sponsorship stops, but can keep campaigning.

Advice from Joe Glanfield:

If you are thinking about doing a proper campaign to a major national or world title, you need to do your finances as though you are running a small business. Have a financial plan and prioritise the things you really need.

It is very easy to waste money just because you have it there. I have seen people get some money to travel who then attend every event in a hectic mess, when they would actually be far better settling and focusing on fewer events.

Likewise people can waste money on equipment simply by buying too many different types of sails and masts; they then have to spend a lot of time testing them and neglect other areas of their sailing.

If you want to find a commercial sponsor, think about what you can do for them rather than the other way round. You can do a lot more than put a sticker on your sail: they can use your name and what you are trying to do to positively influence their brand and to motivate their staff. They can also use you for corporate hospitality events, internal and external competitions (win a day's sailing, etc.). All of these things add a lot to your worth, and therefore to the amount of money you can ask for from a sponsor.

Glossary

Aerobic fitness is the body's ability to deliver oxygen to the muscles, which allows them to work longer and recover more quickly after exercise.

Apparent wind is the actual flow of air acting upon the sail, or the wind as it appears to the sailor. If the boat were stationary, the true and apparent wind would be the same. However as a boat increases in speed the apparent wind becomes progressively faster and further forward than the true wind.

Back is the term given to describe the wind turning in an anti-clockwise direction.

Bear away is to change course away from the wind.

Black Flag. If a black flag has been displayed, no part of a boat's hull, crew or equipment shall be in the triangle formed by the ends of the starting line and the first mark during the minute before her starting signal. If a boat breaks this rule and is identified, she shall be disqualified without a hearing, even if the race is restarted, resailed or rescheduled, but not if it is postponed or abandoned before the starting signal.

Bow down describes a boat sailing upwind pointing as low (pointing as far away from upwind as possible) whilst still maximising ground made to windward.

Chop describes the short steep waves which can have a dramatic effect on reducing boat speed.

Clew is the part of the sail where the leach and the foot of the sail meet (at the far end of the boom).

Converging describes the wind off the land and the wind off the sea coming nearer together.

Cirrus cloud is a thin whispy cloud found 5km above the earth's surface.

Cumulus cloud is a heap of rounded masses (like a fluffy sheep), a low level cloud often seen on a summer's day.

Cover is to position yourself between another boat and the next mark of the course. Upwind this may be to give them dirty air.

Current is the flow of water in a particular direction.

Death roll is where the flow of wind continually switches direction across the sail, causing the boat to roll to windward, then to leeward and back again, often resulting in a swim!

Designed wind is the wind a boat is designed to sail in, at optimum efficiency. This could perhaps be around 14 knots, so the boat can be easily depowered in stronger or lighter winds. However if certain conditions are common at a venue, a boat may be designed for this specific wind.

Diverging describes the wind off the land and the wind off the sea moving further apart.

Eddy is a circular motion which may be found in wind and water.

Exonerate is when a boat takes a penalty for breaking a racing rule. She may for example complete penalty turn(s) or retire from the race.

Foot i) (Noun) The bottom edge of the sail, ii) (Verb) To foot: Sailing the boat fast and low upwind.

Get water is an expression when one boat is given room by another boat to allow her to pass a mark or obstruction.

Going high is sailing upwind of the straight line to the next mark.

Going low is sailing downwind of the straight line to the next mark.

Head is the top of the sail (joining the luff and the leach)

Headed tack. The headed tack is the tack where a boat has to bear away (to keep the same sail settings) as a result of a change in wind direction.

Header is where the wind direction changes (heads), forcing the boat to bear away to keep the sail settings the same.

Heel describes the boat leaning to windward or leeward (i.e. she is no longer flat).

GPS stands for Global positioning system and is a satellite based navigation system.

Kite is another name for spinnaker.

Layer stratus cloud is low level cloud which is a continuous horizontal sheet.

Lay line. The lay line is the straight line which will allow a boat to round the windward mark in the shortest possible time without tacking. This is affected by wind speed, direction and current flows.

Leach is the aft edge of the sail.

Lee bowed. You are lee bowed by a boat close to leeward giving you dirty wind.

Leeward (pronounced "loo-erd") A boat's leeward side is the side that is or, when she is head to wind, was away from the wind. However, when sailing by the lee or directly downwind, her leeward side is the side on which her mainsail lies. The other side is her windward side. When two boats on the same tack overlap, the one on the leeward side of the other is the leeward boat. The other is the windward boat.

Lifted tack. The lifted tack is the tack where a boat has to head up (to keep the same sail settings) as a result of a change in wind direction.

Lifting is where the wind direction changes (lifts), forcing the boat to head up to keep the same sail settings.

Logistics means having the right thing, at the right place, at the right time.

Luff is the forward edging of the sail (from which derives the term "luffing", to go towards where the wind comes from).

Mast rake means the position of the mast forwards or back, which can affect the centre of effort of the sail.

Mean wind is the average wind in terms of speed and direction.

OCS stands for on course side which refers to any part of a boat being on the race course side (OCS) prior to the start. You will have to restart the race, may incur a penalty or possibly be disqualified.

Offshore breeze. A breeze which is coming off the shore (from the land).

Onshore breeze. A breeze which is coming off the land (from the water).

Oscillating breeze is a breeze which is regularly swinging to the left and right (perhaps going to the left for 5 minutes, mean wind direction for 5 minutes, right for 5 minutes back to mean wind direction for 5 minutes and so forth).

Overstanding When the boat is to windward of the layline, this results in her taking a greater time than necessary to reach the windward mark.

Pin end is the port end of the start or finish line, often a buoy.

Pointing (or pinching) describes a boat sailing upwind pointing as high (as close to upwind as possible) whilst still maximising ground made to windward.

Rabbit start One boat, the "rabbit" sails across upwind and the other boats start by crossing behind on the opposite tack. When everyone has started, the rabbit boat tacks, so as to be on the same tack as the rest of the fleet.

Recall is when one or more identified boats are recalled to the starting area (individual recall) or when a race is restarted (general recall).

Reps is short for repetitions – the number of times you repeat an exercise in the gym.

Rolling is when a boat heels to windward then to leeward and back again (or vice versa).

Sailing by the lee is when the flow of wind across the sail is from the leech to the luff of the sail (so the telltales fly towards the mast).

Sailing over is passing someone to windward. You are rolled when a boat to windward gives you dirty wind.

Sailing under is passing someone to leeward.

Sea breeze is an onshore breeze generated by the difference in the temperature between the land and the sea.

Set is a series of repetitions of exercises completed without a rest in between.

Shifty breeze describes a breeze constantly changing direction with no pattern, perhaps caused by the wind coming over some high land or going round tall trees or buildings.

SI stands for Sailing instructions: These are a chronological list for competitors concerning the racing rules of a specific championship or series.

Slam dunk is tacking right on top of someone, to give them the maximum amount of dirty air in a position where they can not immediately tack off.

Soak is where the boat is sailed downwind pointing as low (pointing as close to dead downwind as possible) whilst still maximising ground made to leeward.

Strategy is the way you would sail around a course as quickly as possible in the absence of other boats.

Swell describes the long rolling waves which do not break. These can often be surfed downwind.

Tack i) (Noun) is the part of the sail where the luff meets the foot. ii) (Noun) a boat is on a tack, starboard or port, corresponding to her windward side. iii) (Verb) To tack is to go from one close hauled course to another when sailing upwind.

Tactics is the way you react to the boats around you.

Team racing involves two teams (of two or more identical boats) sailing against one another. The winning team is determined by the total number of points scored by all boats of that team.

Telltales are pieces of wool or ribbon attached to the sail or stay, to indicate the wind direction.

Tides are the rising (flooding) and falling (ebbing) of the Earth's ocean surface twice each day caused by the tidal forces of the moon and the sun acting on the oceans.

Topography is the shape and surface of the surrounding area.

Transit is a line going through two fixed points.

Transom is the stern of the boat.

Vang lever pushes down on the boom to increase leach tension (as opposed to a kicker which pulls down on the boom).

Veer is the term used to describe the wind turning in a clockwise direction.

VMG stands for velocity made good (total distance travelled in a certain direction in a certain time).

Wind bend is where the wind gradually changes direction to the left or right over a distance, often caused by topography.

Windward A boat's windward side is the side that is or, when she is head to wind, was towards the wind. However, when sailing by the lee or directly downwind, her windward side is the opposite side to which her mainsail lies. The other side is her leeward side. When two boats on the same tack overlap, the one on the windward side of the other is the windward boat. The other is the leeward boat.

Index

Aerobic exercise   212
Apparent wind   172, 175, 180–181, 184, 185

Bannister, Roger   220
boat handling xiv   12, 58–72, 75
  advice   72
  changing gear   69–71
  dartboard xiv
  gybes   62–69
    exercises   65–69
  steering, minimising   58
  surfing   59–60, 113, 120
  tacks   62–69
    exercises   65–69
  turns, top and bottom   59–62
boat preparation   244–251
  advice   250–251
  boat work, dealing with   243–244, 247–249
  checklist   245–249
  foil preparation   245
  how prepared is the boat?   244
    common mistakes   246
  hull   244, 247, 248, 250
  repairs   244, 246
  rig   244
  sails   10, 246
  spars   246
  spares   245, 251
  sun damage   246

  toolkit   34, 251
boat speed see reaching; running; upwind boat
    speed
body weight   16, 22, 191, 210–214
  advice   214
  dieting, yo-yo   210
  gaining   16, 212
  losing   210, 211, 212
  maintaining and recovering   210
  budget   256

checklists   13–15, 249–251
clouds cirrus   151
  cumulus   28, 149
coaches   6, 29, 229, 254
communication   18, 20, 165, 175, 237
concentration   18, 165, 219, 223, 234–241
  advice   241
  focus, maintaining   237–240
    written notes   238
  focusing on boat speed   237
  mental energies, factors which decrease   233,
    235–236
  mental fatigue   235
  mental fitness   240
  mental stamina   234
  peak   240
costs see finance
current   46, 47, 94, 95, 97, 98, 105, 107–109, 116

dartboard, blank (appendix)
  how to complete xiii
  of chapters (appendix)
death roll 178, 182
diary *see* racing log
diet 20, 200–208 *see also* body weight
  advice 208
  calories 200, 203–211
  carbohydrates 201, 202, 204
  fats 203
  food diary 207
  foods, necessary 204–205
  for health 206, 211
    suggestions 204–206
  hydration 10, 204, 206, 212, 234, 241
  meals, timing of 205, 207
  minerals 204
  nutritional labelling 201
  protein 202
  salt 203
  suggestions 204, 205, 206
  supplements 204
  vitamins 204
  water 10, 206, 234

equipment *see* technology

finance 254–260
  advice 260
  budget 256
  campaigning 256–258
    cost, typical 255
    dartboard 254, 257
    investment to campaign, value of 257
  sailing, true cost 254–255
  sponsorship 258–260
finish, rule definition 122–123
finish, rules used aggressively 137–138
fitness 16 *see also* preparation,
        self: physical 187–197
  advice 197
  body weight *see* body weight 209
  dartboards 189, 190, 191

four 'Ss' 188–189
  improving 192, 211
    for all sailors 195–196
    heart rate monitoring 193, 194, 211
    hiking 193–194
    pushing to next level 193
    training for 49er crew 194
    training for Keelboats 189, 195
    training for Laser hiker 191, 193, 194
    warm up 192, 193
    weight training 196, 211, 227
  need for 191
  peaking at the correct time 11–13, 188
  race 5, 10, 11, 12
  what is it? 188
flights, booking 18, 19
focus, maintaining 235–241
  written notes 226, 227, 231, 238, 240
focusing on boat speed 237
foil preparation 245
foils 161
footing 159, 163, 164
49er 114, 175, 185, 188, 194, 251

Gantt chart 14
Garda, Lake 113
Glanfield, Joe 154, 165, 208, 214, 221, 231,
        241, 258, 260
goal setting 2–7, 231
  advice 7
  importance of 2
goals
  long-term 3–4, 5–6
  medium-term 3–4, 5
  short-term 3–4, 5, 7
  SMART 2–3
  timed 3–4
Goodison, Paul 7, 30, 54–55, 72, 91, 186, 191
Google Earth 25
GPS (Global Positioning System) 35
gybes 59, 62–65, 68, 109–113, 168, 173, 180
  exercises 65–68
gybing on the shifts 68, 110

heart rate monitoring   193, 194, 228
Hiscocks, Simon   16, 34–36, 117, 142, 175, 250–251
hull preparation   247, 248, 250
hydration   10, 206, 208, 212, 234, 241

Keelboat   195
kicker use   52, 62, 157, 168, 178, 179

Laser   114, 159, 178, 181, 186, 188–191, 193
Laylines   59, 82, 83, 97, 98, 103–105, 113, 115, 140, 170
Leebow   163
Logistics   18–20

mark, going straight for   84, 85, 86
mark rounding   81–90
marks, rules used aggressively   137–138
marks, rules used defensively   139–141
mast bend and rake   35, 156, 157, 158, 159, 168
mental attitude   216–221 see also preparation, self: mental
  advice   221
  aggression   217
  correct, importance of   216–218
  excuses   218, 221
  negatives, dealing with   216, 217–218
  pressure, handling   216–218
  relaxation   11, 236, 240
    rational analysis and   220
  relaxation techniques   219
    affirmations   220
    detachment and mental imagery   219
    keywords   219–220
    pattern breaking   220
    reframe   219
mental energies, factors which decrease   235, 236
mental fatigue   234
mental fitness   236
mental stamina   234
meteorology   144–154 see also weather and wind entries
  advice   154

Olympic classes, venues for   21
Optimist   111
organisation   13, 15 see also preparation, self   165, 247–251, 254–260

planning   13–15, 16, 247–251
Plastic Padding   246
'pointing'   161–164, 168
Polar S610 heart rate monitor   194
preparation, self   10–16
  advice   16
  checklists   13–15
  diet   16, 19 see also diet
  how prepared are you?   10–11
  and kit   11, 12, 15, 16
  mental   10–11, 12 see also mental attitude   216–221, 234–236
  peaking at the correct time   11–13, 188
  physical   10, 11, 12, 16 see also fitness
  registration for race   11
  relaxation   11, 240
  unexpected happenings   11, 16
  and water conditions, different   21
  weight   16, 22 see also body weight   209
preparation, venue   18–30
  advice   30
  communication   18, 20
  flight booking   18, 19
  logistics   18–20
  practising   30, 91
  tidal knowledge   22, 24
  weather patterns   21–22
protesting   128–130
public speaking   259

race analysis   229–230
race signals   121, 127
races, registration for   11
racing log   224–231
  advice   231
  heart rate graph   228 see also heart rate monitoring
  race analysis   229–230

racing log (*continued*)
  reasons for keeping   224–226
  records, good, how to keep   226–228
  rig tuning diary   228
  weight training diary   227
reaching   168–175
  advice   175
  average speed, keeping high   171
  dartboard   173
  going for speed   171–174
  kicker use   167–168
  rig set-up   168
  'soaking' low   169, 170, 173
  tuning runs   173
relaxation   11, 218–220, 234, 236 *see also*
      mental attitude
rig preparation   245–246
rig set-up
  for reaching   168
  for running   178–180
  at start   39
  for upwind boat speed   156–161
    mast bend and rake   35, 156–159
    sail fundamentals   156–157
    unstayed rig   158–159
rig tuning diary   226
rigging, checking   34
rules   120–142
  advice   142
  aggressive use   137
    finishing   137, 138
    at marks   136
    slotting in to leeward   137
    starting   134, 139
  basics   120–136
  defensive use   139–141
    double tack   139
    'slam dunk'   140
    starting   139
    windward mark approach   140–141
  definitions   120–136
    abandoned race   121
    clear ahead/astern   122

finish   131
interested party   123
keep clear   123
leeward   124, 142
marks   125
obstructions   126
overlap   122
party   123, 127
postponed race   127
proper course   128
protest   128–130
racing   131
room   131, 132
rule book   120, 131–133
start   134
tack   134–135
two-length zone   135–136
windward   124, 142
race signals   121, 127
running   178–186
  advice   186
  apparent wind sailing   184–185
  downwind tack   180
  kicker   178, 179
  rig set-up   178
  sailing by the lee   181, 184, 185
    'death roll'   182
    downwind by the waves   182–183
    flow of wind over sail   181
  telltales   179, 180, 181
  waves, heading up and bearing away
      from   179

sail fundamentals, upwind   156–159
  sailing by the lee   181, 184, 185
sails, preparation   10
S.I. (sailing instructions)   11, 133
skiffs, asymmetric   175 *see also* 49er
Skype   20
'slam dunk'   140
'soaking'   169, 170, 173
sponsorship   256, 260
start, rabbit   65

start, rule definition   134
start, rules used aggressively   137–138
start, rules used defensively   139–141
starting   38–55, 134
    acceleration   38–43, 53
        three boat trigger pulling   41–43
    advice   54–55
    distance   38–45
    line position   45–52
    protecting your space   52–53
    remembering the rest of the race   48–53
    rig set-up   39
    tide considerations   45–48
    time   38–41
        buoy to leeward   40–41
        buoy to windward   40
    transits   49–50
    wave conditions   47
    wind considerations   45–48
steering, minimising   58
steering upwind   159–161
strategic considerations dartboard   96
strategy   94–117
    advice   117
    and tide   97–99
    dartboard   96
    practising at venue   30, 91
    what is it?   94–96
strategy, downwind   107–116
    gybing on the shifts   110
    local topography   113, 117
    positioning   111–112
    pressure differences   112–113
    safe option   115–116
    sailing on favoured side of the run   9
    sailing shortest course   116
    sailing straight line on a reach   108, 116
    surfing   59–62, 113, 114, 120
    wave conditions   113–115, 168, 179, 181,
        183, 186
strategy-reaching   170, 171
strategy, upwind   97–107
    current direction   97–99

playing the percentages   106–110
water friction   105–106
wind variations   99–105, 117
    sailing for the pressure   101, 102
    staying towards centre of course   100–101
    tacking on the shifts   100–101
    wind bend   103
    wind shift, expected   103–105
surfing   59–61, 113

tacking on the shifts dartboards xv, xvi   27,
        100–101
tacks   62–69
    exercises   5, 65–69
tactical considerations dartboard   75
tactics   59, 74–91
    advice   91
    boat-to-boat   74–75
    dartboard   75
    key ideas   90
tactics, downwind   84–90
    going low   86
    leeward mark rounding   84, 87, 88, 89
    mark, going straight for   84, 85, 86
    overlap to windward   88
    windward mark, after   87, 88, 89
tactics, reaching   170, 171
tactics, upwind   76–84
    attack and defence   76, 77, 78
    consistency   81
    cover   77, 79
    defence and attack   76, 77, 78
    leading the fleet   78–79
    mark rounding   83, 84, 85, 86
    sailing your own race   82, 83
    slowing someone down   80, 81
team, fixed   5–6
team racing   74
team tasks   38–39
technology   32–36
    advice   34–36
    changes, recording   33
    perfect solution, finding   33

technology (*continued*)
  simplicity   33
  trends, keeping up with   32
  what can assist   35
telltales   146, 160, 179, 180, 181
tidal knowledge   22, 24
tide when starting   46–48
tides and strategy   22, 91, 94, 95, 106
time on the water   225
toolkit   14–15, 34, 249
topography   113, 117, 152
Tornado   111, 258
transits   49–50, 116
tuning   156
turns, top and bottom   59–62

upwind boat speed   156–165
  advice   165
  body movement   160–161
  centre of effort/resistance   156, 159
  kicker use   157
  making the boat 'foot'   159, 164
  making the boat 'point'   159, 161–163
  steering   159–161

venue preparation   *see* preparation, venue
VMG (velocity made good)   162, 163, 172, 174

wave conditions   47, 159, 168, 179, 181,
    183, 186
weather forecasts, understanding   144–145
  boundary layer   147

examples   146–147
heating effect of sun   145–146
wind   147
weather forecasts, using   148–152
  advice   154
  breezes   149
  clouds   149–151
  fronts   150, 151
  local effects   152
  sea breezes   149, 153
  stable air   149
  wind   149, 150
    as forecast   148
weather information sources   144–145
weather patterns   21–22 *see also* wind patterns
weight training   196, 212, 227
wind and forecasts   144–145, 149
wind and strategy   *see* strategy: upwind, wind
    variations
wind bend   103
wind data   23
wind patterns   25–29 *see also* weather patterns
wind, apparent   172, 175, 184, 185
  convergent   26–27, 101–102, 111
  divergent   26, 27, 111, 112, 148
  offshore breeze   27–28, 145, 152, 153
  sea breeze   28–29, 103, 104, 115, 152, 153
  wind parallel to land   26–27, 101, 102,
    111, 112
wind when starting   45–48
windguru   144
zone, being in the   240

With thanks to A. Thatcher for compilation of this index.

RACE SIGNALS

The meanings of visual and sound signals are stated below. An arrow pointing up or down (↑ ↓) means that a visual signal is displayed or removed. A dot (•) means a sound; five short dashes (– – – – –) mean repetitive sounds; a long dash (—) means a long sound. When a visual signal is displayed over a class flag, the signal applies only to that class.

Postponement Signals

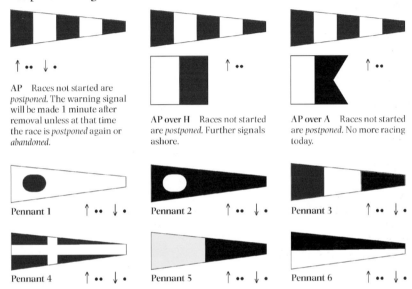

AP Races not started are *postponed.* The warning signal will be made 1 minute after removal unless at that time the race is *postponed* again or *abandoned.*

AP over H Races not started are *postponed.* Further signals ashore.

AP over A Races not started are *postponed.* No more racing today.

Pennant 1   ↑ •• ↓ •

Pennant 2   ↑ •• ↓ •

Pennant 3   ↑ •• ↓ •

Pennant 4   ↑ •• ↓ •

Pennant 5   ↑ •• ↓ •

Pennant 6   ↑ •• ↓ •

AP over a numeral pennant 1–6 *Postponement* of 1–6 hours from the scheduled starting time.

Abandonment Signals

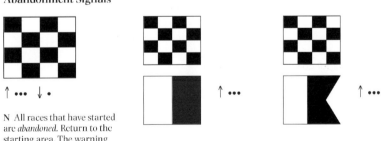

N All races that have started are *abandoned.* Return to the starting area. The warning signal will be made 1 minute after removal unless at that time the race is *abandoned* again or *postponed.*

N over H All races are *abandoned.* Further signals ashore.

N over A All races are *abandoned.* No more racing today.

Preparatory Signals

↑ • ↓ —

P   Preparatory signal.

↑ • ↓ —

I   Rule 30.1 is in effect.

↑ • ↓ —

Z   Rule 30.2 is in effect.

↑ • ↓ —

Black flag.   Rule 30.3 is in effect.

Recall Signals

↑ •

X   Individual recall.

↑ •• ↓ •

First Substitute   General recall. The warning signal will be made 1 minute after removal.

Course Change Signals

↑ ••

S   The course has been shortened. Rule 32.2 is in effect.

– – – – –

C   The position of the next *mark* has been changed.

Other Signals

↑ •

L   Ashore: A notice to competitors has been posted.

Afloat: Come within hail or follow this boat.

– – – – –

M   The object displaying this signal replaces a missing *mark*.

↑ •

Y   Wear personal buoyancy.

(no sound)

Blue flag or shape. This race committee boat is in position at the finishing line.

Blank dartboard for you to photocopy and use. Good Luck!

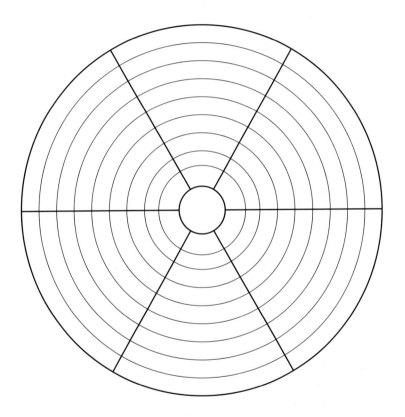

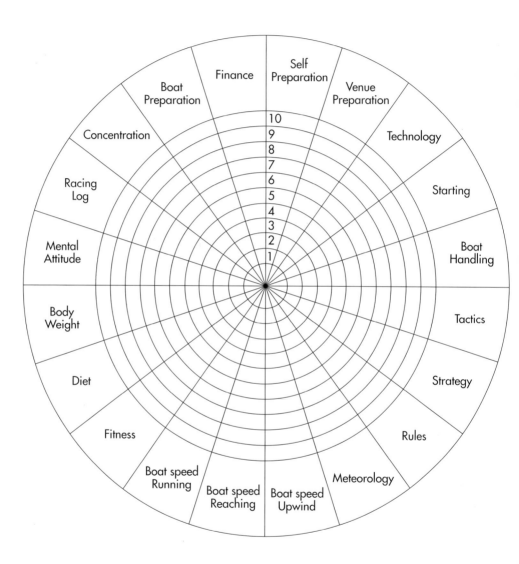